CW00519836

Two and
Two Halves
...and a Dog

A BLACKBURN CHILDHOOD

JOAN POTTER

Two and
Two Halves
...and a Dog

A BLACKBURN CHILDHOOD

First published in Great Britain in 2009 by
The Breedon Books Publishing Company Limited
Breedon House, 3 The Parker Centre,
Derby, DE21 4SZ.

This edition published in Great Britain in 2012 by The Derby Books Publishing
Company Limited, 3 The Parker Centre, Derby, DE21 4SZ.

© Joan Potter, 2009

All Rights Reserved. No part of this publication may be reproduced, stored in a
retrieval system, or transmitted in any form, or by any means, electronic, mechanical,
photocopying, recording or otherwise without the prior permission in writing of the
copyright holders, nor be otherwise circulated in any form or binding or cover other
than in which it is published and without a similar condition being imposed on the
subsequent publisher.

ISBN 978-1-78091-167-0

Contents

In memory of my parents and my brother,
Doris, Victor and David Ryan.

Acknowledgements

Among the numerous people whose generous assistance has furthered the completion of this book I am particularly grateful to the following: Patsy Colvin, Pat and John Dixon, Liz Jopling, Mary Miller, Hazel Pidcock, Jean Pritchett, Liz Renshaw, Barbara Riding, Peter Ryan, Carol Walker, Peter Warren and Hilary Withers for recollections and photographs; Chris Catherall, Helen Duxbury, Robert Gambles, Ian Maxwell, Ruth Shackleton, Peter Worden, Hillary Healey (Headteacher of St Silas' School) and her staff, particularly Sam Patel, Janice Ward and Janet Wilson, Janet Clegg (Clerk to the Parish of St Michael and St John, Clitheroe), Andrew Rice-Oxley and Diana Rushton and the staff of Blackburn Library Community History Section for help with research; John Kennedy of Liverpool University Continuing Education Department, Gabrielle Rollinson of Southport College and Professor Robert Sheppard, Ailsa Cox and my fellow students at Edge Hill University, especially Laurence Doherty, Carol Fenlon, Cyrus Ferguson and Trevor Williams, for comment and encouragement; Gill Enstone for comment, encouragement and proofreading, and my husband, Stuart Potter, for his unfailing patience, assistance and support.

Changing Stations

There was nothing more to say. The last door slammed, the whistle shrilled, and with a piercing hoot and a hiss of steam billowing under the station canopy, the train roared and rumbled into motion.

'Bye, Mum, bye,' I called, peering into the swirling smuts, soot filling my nostrils and my eyes beginning to sting. 'See you soon.'

'Let us know when you get there,' she responded, then something else which only the wind heard. A surge of power, a curve in the line and she was gone, a solitary figure on the station platform, watching her last child leave.

I hauled up the window, struggling to secure the leather strap on its brass button as I did so, swung my suitcase onto the netting rack above my head, flung the despised school gabardine on top of it and settled back into my corner of the third-class carriage. Clackety-clack, clackety-clack, clackety-clack, the stations whizzed by – Lower Darwen, Hoddlesden, Darwen, Entwistle – but I was blind to them. Excitement had carried me through so far, but now there was more than smoke stinging my eyes. I avoided the glances of my fellow passengers by pretending an interest in the sepia prints fixed below the racks, advertising the holiday resorts of Blackpool, Morecambe and Southport, then stared out into the rain.

There were two other people in my compartment. Much as I would have preferred my own company I knew better than to get into an empty one, or one without women, but there was always the prospect of having to talk. Today was no exception.

'Off to Manchester, love?' I could hear the concern in the voice, and my already unsteady insides took another lurch. But I was not going to cry, to disgrace myself in public. Forced to meet her sympathetic gaze I found a well-built, middle-aged lady smiling at me from the far end of the seat, facing a younger woman who looked to me like her married daughter. 'Someone meeting you, is there?'

'My dad,' I muttered discouragingly, and then, manners overcoming shyness, 'After that I'm going to Sheffield.'

'Oh, you off to school then?'

School! That confusion again. I was sick of it from some of my parents' friends who obviously thought I should have gone out to work at 14. I was embarrassed by their questions and sometimes wished I had been sent out to work, so that I would not have seemed different.

'University,' I declared. 'It's not the same.' Her daughter saved me by putting an end to the questions.

'We're going to Manchester too, shopping. Our Eileen's getting wed soon and Mum wants to get her something special. We're going to start at Lewis's and then maybe even go to Kendal's,' she explained.

'Well I don't know about that, love, except to gawp at all them export only goods in the tunnel between the shops if they're still there. What about Marshall and Snelgroves?'

To my relief they became absorbed in their own conversation and I turned to the window again, leaning my head against the rough upholstery to avoid the chill from the glass. Soon their chatter was no more than comfortable background noise mixed with the rhythm of the rails as the landscape I knew flashed by in a blur of speed and rain. What would it be like, I wondered, this new life of mine? How would I fare? Was I clever enough? Would I make friends? Among roughly 700 freshers, about 600 of them boys, I would know only Hilary, who had a place in the women's hall of residence, far across the city from the digs I was to share with four strangers.

My stomach stirred as fear and anticipation of the unknown combined with the wrench of leaving home, but despite everything, I recognised that I was glad to be getting away. Not only was I ready for change, but also the shadow that my uncle's death had cast over the household had become too much for me. I envisaged a new world, a chance to start again, unaware of my childhood trailing on the tracks beside me.

Departure Points

The war gave me a largely absent father until I was six. Prior to joining the RAF he spent his days at work in Preston and his nights patrolling the streets or at the observation post in Billinge Wood as an ARP warden. He volunteered in 1941 but was deferred until 1942, when he sailed to South Africa for flight training almost immediately. By then he was 31, my mother 38, my brother David five and I almost two, so my earliest memory of him, indeed one of my earliest memories altogether, is of arriving home on leave a year or so later.

It disturbs me that my first remembered encounter with him was far from a success. I did not understand who this man was or why he was staying in our house, even though he had been figuring in my prayers as long as he had been away. My mother, brought up a Non-conformist and married to a lapsed Catholic, never seemed particularly religious, but every night during the war, before she turned out the bedroom light and went downstairs, the three of us would chorus, 'God bless Daddy.' Later I remember adding, 'and you as well'.

My father had brought me home two beautiful dolls, German ones, which opened and closed their eyes. They were something very special in those days but so lovely and so different from my other tattered toys that, though I looked at them sometimes, I had no desire to play with them, then or ever. When I cleared out my parents' home half a century later I found them in the tallboy, just where my father hid his service revolver when he came home on leave, as David had once discovered and shown me. The dolls were still lying with closed eyes in their original brown cardboard boxes; coffins for dreams.

My father also brought home some bananas which, like most children, my brother and I had never seen. David tried to eat one without peeling it, and even when we had been shown what to do, and despite the fact that we were prepared to eat most things since the alternative was hunger, we really did not like them. Young as I was I could feel my father's disappointment   I still carry the image of that bunch of bananas lying rejected on his kitbag in the passage, matching the yellow distemper on the wall behind them.

'In the passage' – now there is an expression from my past. My parents had begun their married life in a standard house about a mile away, at No. 24 Brighton Terrace, but soon moved. Following a serious fire they rented one of a pair of non-matching cottages which had formerly housed the coachman and other servants of a cotton magnate's mansion, so it was far from standard. What we called the passage was just that: a way through the house from the front door straight into the kitchen from which the back door opened into the stable-yard. That was our main entrance. Only post and papers entered through the front door, and that only because it held the letterbox.

The stables were empty of horses but our living room window framed a view of a stable door, a grey slate roof, a blank brick wall and a corner of the coal shed. Dismal? Well, up to a point, but it was redeemed by a patch of sky backing the ancient horse chestnuts which towered over the lane down the side of the house. In winter they offered a sinister, shifting pattern of branches against the night sky; in summer a glorious mass of green decked with white candles and eventually, in autumn, a ready supply of conkers. Then there were the birds that came for the crumbs and bacon rind left on the coal shed roof – and the cats that came for the birds.

The stable-yard itself was a roofed area about 20ft by 30, which stretched across the back of both houses to form a high, open-ended shed into which our back steps led. Roller shutters in the opposite wall closed off a similar sized area where cars, immobilised by the petrol shortage, occupied the space once filled by coaches. At the far end of the shed the carriage-drive led to the front of the mansion; at our end it finished in a small open area in front of the living room window, cut off from the lane, Troy Back or Bank as it was then variously known, by a high wooden gate. Thus we had a share of a secure, covered area, which provided the space our house lacked. As I grew this giant umbrella, shared by my mother through the open kitchen door, protected my pram, my play pen and my early games. Here, too, washing was boiled and strung on the line, fire-wood chopped and household equipment cobbled together or repaired.

On one side of the passage were the staircase up to the bathroom and the two bedrooms in the roof-space, and a door to the space under the stairs. On the other side were the doors to the living room and the front room. From the latter the view was restricted not by buildings, but by a terraced bank of garden which climbed the steep slope from the retaining wall a few feet from the front door. The top, about 20ft away, was level with the front bedroom window, but that never seemed to matter. The sunken front doorway was a sun-trap and the lowest terrace a shifting sea of bluebells in spring. Rambling red roses clothed the high wall of the lane to the side of it, in front of which grew senecio and lilac, both the subject of annual squabbling between my parents.

'Vic!' my mother would cry, seeing him returning the shears to the coal shed and rushing to the front door to look at the massacred shrubs, 'you've been at the lilac again. There'll be no flowers next year. You must have killed the other bush this time. I do wish you'd leave them alone.'

'They'll be all right,' he would reply calmly, and every year he chopped, my mother protested and the plants flourished.

In summer, even though it was our main source of heating and only source of hot water from its back boiler, the fire in the black-leaded kitchen range in the living room often remained unlit. Then we seemed to live at the front door, seduced by light and warmth. On dry days the wide, flat top of the retaining wall was my father's potting shed, workbench and even desk, as well as a play table for me and David. Thinking of the house now, all I see and feel is sunshine. The light through the open front door is picking out the pattern in the carpet, my mother sings in the kitchen and bees drone in the rose-scented air. I drift in peace and security.

Sadly for my mother, much as she loved her home it was always too isolated for her, cruelly so during the war. Accustomed to the company of friends and family, she found herself tied to the house by two young children, with her husband away, and everyone she knew on the other side of town. Her widowed father was busy with his tobacconists shop, her sister was a two-mile walk away with a husband at home to look after as well as child of her own, and her best friend had married and moved to Padiham. Even air-raids saw her alone as there were no shelters nearby; we simply huddled under the table when the sirens wailed. Nor was there a friendly group of neighbours to support her. They were mostly too distant and we had little to do with our only close neighbours, the family in the adjoining cottage. I do not remember the father, who I think was away most of the time, but I recall his wife as kind, if rather rough and loud. I think she may have thought my mother snobbish; Mother certainly thought her common, but they co-existed well enough and David and I played happily with the three sons, though never in each other's houses. The nearest we got to inside was their cellar, an exciting – and forbidden – chilly blackness. It was entered from outside through a rotting door at the bottom of a flight of stone steps from which emanated a nose-wrinkling smell of damp and decay, backed by the continuous plop of dripping water. If I passed the steps on my own, I always ran.

We were never desperately poor during those war years: never without food, clothing or shelter, but with little money to provide them as my mother struggled to keep the three of us on my father's Air Force pay. She scrimped and saved and sewed and survived, a shining example of the government's Make Do and Mend campaign. So resourceful was she that I was able to enter – and win – an infants' fancy dress competition. She added a few pins and a tape-measure to my normal outfit and fastened a label to me bearing the campaign slogan.

Mother made sure we had treats, too, though we soon learnt not to ask for things, or whine for what we could not have and make her cross. I can hear her now, 'Stop that, or I'll give you something to cry for,' or 'Pull a face like that and the wind'll change so you'll have it forever.' Nevertheless, we never went without presents for birthdays or Christmas, though frequently they were something we needed anyway, often clothing, almost all of which she made. She spent hour after hour in the front room, hunched over the sewing machine or cutting out material on the floor, only switching on our alternative source of heating, a wonky, one-bar electric radiator, if she needed to finish something off when the temperature had sunk lower than she could bear.

Our belief in Father Christmas was preserved by artificial socks made from string and crêpe paper, refilled annually with simple toys and sweets from our ration, bought from Grandad's shop. One year mine contained a baby doll about two inches high, together with a red and white plastic cradle to rock it in, which became a favourite toy, appealing to me in a way that the fancy German dolls had failed to do. We knew that Mother was the provider of any other presents we had since, unless we were in school, we went wherever she did as there was no one to look after us. One year someone nearby advertised second-hand toys for sale and the three of us stumbled the quarter of a mile up the lane in the blackout to a house near Mile End Row. Mother hesitated outside the door, finally knocked and in we went, to a warm welcome, a glowing fire and a floor covered with toys for us to choose from. We were even allowed to play for a while with the ones we could not have. Eventually we went home with a bagatelle game to share and another present each. That was a good Christmas. Another year Mother heard there was a shop that had some dolls' prams for sale. Knowing that I longed for one she left David at school, took me to her sister's, rushed into town and queued for an hour and a half, only to see the last one sold just ahead of her.

I always wanted to do what my big brother did, which included going to school. As far as I knew David, nearly four years my senior, had always done so, since my earliest and most regular outings were the half-mile walks I made with my mother accompanying him there and back. For once I got my way, so in September 1943, at the age of three, I, too, became a St Silas's pupil, or rather a St Silas' pupil, as punctuation and authority insisted in those days, but not in the building where David had started.

When war was declared the school premises were requisitioned for an ARP first aid post and, while the juniors were temporarily accommodated nearby in Leamington Road Baptist Church, the infants were housed in the Parish Rooms on Preston New Road, which is where my brother went. With the decreased threat of air raids the school was handed back, apart from one classroom, so I began my formal education in a back room on the ground floor of the main school in Clematis Street, which I thought a wonderful place.

There was a huge box of sand along one wall to climb into and grovel about in when I arrived each morning, a seesaw – or rather a swingboat-shaped metal frame with green canvas seats, which not only rocked but also shifted across the floor with a satisfying scrape – together with heaps of rag-books, lots of coloured plasticine which left its smell on my fingers all day, and slates to scribble and draw on endlessly. Paper did not figure in our activities. It was in short supply and far too precious to be wasted on toddlers. Brightness and colour were also in short supply, as the room itself offered little: rough wooden floor, brown dado, green paint and grimy arched windows way above head height, with soiled hangman's ropes dangling from the opening sections.

The brightest aspect was the infant teacher, Miss Holden. A peaches and cream girl, worlds away from the anxious or elderly adults who surrounded us, we loved her unreservedly. I have never forgotten what she said to me as I lay howling on the floor, having tipped my tiny chair too far back on two legs and banged my head on the wall as I fell off it. 'That,' she declared, 'will teach you to sit on your chair properly!' And I still thought she was wonderful.

School also gave me other children to play with. Apart from my cousin Christine, who was between me and David in age, a frequent visitor to our house and the main companion of my early childhood, my regular playmates were mainly boys: David and the three next door. The exception was Caroline, who was to remain my best friend for years. Our mothers became friends at the school gates as they waited for our older brothers and often, on fine days, once they appeared we went to Corporation Park together. At first Caroline and I were pushed in our prams, but soon we were stretching through the railings round the lake to feed the ducks, being bored by the plants in the conservatory while enjoying its warmth, and polishing our knickers sliding down the pink granite erratic on the Broad Walk. By the time we went to school we had graduated to playing on the swings and soaking ourselves and each other in trying to drink from the water-fountain beside them, and we were very happy to be there together. Though we were parted when Caroline's mother died and she lived for a time with an aunt, we resumed our friendship on her return but never talked about her absence. My mother told me not to bother her by asking questions.

Other than going to school, my outings were usually uneventful tram rides into town with my mother to visit my grandad in Victoria Street, to go to the shops or, more commonly, the market. Two of these excursions were, however, far too memorable as early cracks in my shell of security. The first occurred in Woolworths, the biggest shop in town, which was cheap and always crowded. Old enough to be out of reins, when Mother let go of my hand at one of the counters, I was free. Bored, I squirmed off through the drab curtain of skirts and bags to see what I could find, standing on tiptoe in an effort to see what lay on the wooden counters and then struggling back to clutch my mother's coat – only it was not hers.

'Stop that, love,' and a strange hand brushed me away.

Bewildered, I pushed past legs and coats, tunnelled between bodies and counters. Where was my mother? Was that her coat, her shoes? The customers were too busy searching for goods they could afford to notice me. The assistants were out of reach in their own squares of counters, serving and taking money. Tears came with fear. The door – perhaps she'd be waiting for me by the door. I managed to find it and stood there, scared and weeping.

'What's up, love? Where's your mum?'

'I don't know,' I sobbed. 'In there.' The woman stood upright and followed my pointing finger, putting down her shopping bag and tugging at her headscarf as she gazed into the crowd.

'Don't you worry. Stop crying now. We'll just wait while she comes out.' We waited. My crying turned to snivelling and then stopped, but there was no sign of my mother. My tears began again. 'She must have gone home to look for you. Where d'you live?'

'Billinge End.'

'Billinge End. I don't know where that is. Did you come on t'tram? D'you know t'way back?' I nodded, unable to speak through my sobs. 'Here's a penny. Go on home. Your mum'll be there,' and with that she went on her way.

Left alone, just turned three and used to doing as I was told, I set off, clutching the proffered penny. Along to the Boulevard I went, onto the tram and off at the terminus, not interested for once in crashing the seat backs over to face the way we had come or watching the conductor swing the trolley round to the other end with his long pole. On I trotted, fear forgotten, across Billinge End Road, then Preston New Road, along the drive, under the shed – and found the back door locked. Confused and miserable, I huddled on the back step where I was found eventually by Mrs Gill. I sat in her house for what seemed like hours until a knock at the door found me sobbing again, into the arms of my frantic mother who had searched everywhere in the shop before finally going to the police. It was a long time before I strayed again, and the next incident in town which disturbed and frightened me was completely different.

Mother and I were again out shopping while David was at school. I was skipping along cheerfully because we had been in the Co-op Emporium, where I could bounce on the sprung floor upstairs and watch the little canisters carrying payments and change from counters to cashier whizzing along their wires over my head. I was glad to be out of the Co-op lift, too, which both thrilled and frightened me as it moved slowly up and down the gloomy stairwell, black greasy ropes looping in the dark shaft and metal gates clanging at intervals to cage and un-cage passengers. So I smiled happily at one of our neighbours who crossed the street to speak to my mother, but oddly, she ignored me.

'Oh, Mrs Ryan. I've got a message for you from Mr Ryan.'

'From Vic? But I don't –'

'Don't worry. He's all right, but he landed unofficially at Salmesbury this afternoon and hitched a lift home.'

'He's home!' Mother sounded excited. 'Oh, do excuse me. I must go.' But we didn't go.

'I'm sorry,' Mrs Haydock went on, 'but he came to see if we knew where you were and asked us to tell you he'd called. He waited as long as he could but only had a short time and had to go back. I'm so very sorry.'

She was gone and we began to cross Town Hall Street, but I was puzzled. My mother was moving very slowly and hurting my hand. I looked up, complaining, but shock silenced me. My mother was crying.

I had seen too little of my father to miss him. His place was often filled for me and David by his two much younger and more carefree brothers. Still schoolboys when I was born, attending St Mary's College in Blackburn despite having moved to Clitheroe, they frequently came for tea after school. They were the ones who played with me for hours, swung me through the air and tossed me from one to the other, heedless of my mother's protests. I adored them, particularly the younger one, Herbert, and was puzzled and upset when they stopped coming. As usual I sought help from my brother.

'David, why don't Uncle Frank and Uncle Herbert come any more?'

'They've joined up.'

'What's that mean?'

'They've joined the Air Force, stupid,' he snapped. 'They'll be back,' and he ran off, looking miserable and leaving me still confused. At the end of the war, when only Uncle Frank started coming again, I was even more confused. This time, I questioned him.

'Your Uncle Herbert's missing,' he said softly. 'He was lost in an aeroplane over Italy.' He paused, then swung me up into the air as usual. 'Come on. Time to find your mother.' I was content. I had been lost myself but someone had always found me.

When I eventually understood that 'missing' meant dead, I could not accept it. I began to worry when I was naughty in case Uncle Herbert was up in Heaven watching me, but at the same time it was years before I stopped praying for it to be a mistake and admitted to myself that my beloved uncle would never walk through the door again. I was five when he died, less than three weeks before the war ended; he was 19.

I have several of his books including a copy of Palgrave's *Golden Treasury* in which he had marked some of the poems, including the following sonnet:

Remember me when I am gone away,
Gone far away into the silent land;
When you can no more hold me by the hand,
Nor I half turn to go yet turning stay.
Remember me when no more day by day
You tell me of our future that you planned;
Only remember me, you understand
It will be late to counsel then or pray.
Yet if you should forget me for a while
And afterwards remember, do not grieve:
For if the darkness and corruption leave
A vestige of the thoughts that once I had,
Better by far you should forget and smile
Than that you should remember and be sad.
(Christina Rossetti)

Return Tickets

Travelling in wartime with two small children must have been frightful, but we travelled at least twice to be close to my father. My first memory is a blurred impression of crowded trains, strange men helping with our luggage and a dismal bed and breakfast place somewhere near Snaith, perpetually wreathed in fog. Perhaps this was subsequent to the incident recounted in the following extract from a recording made for my father's retirement ceremony in 1975. The words are those of his former pilot and lifelong friend, Eric Kimber:

> *Of course, our other memorable trip was our night operational flight over Germany when we lost an engine there and had a long trek back with Jerry searchlights picking us up, and we created a long-distance record of 600 miles on one engine. I think the whole of the British Isles must have moved south while we were on this flight, as we took off from Essex and landed in Yorkshire, which we didn't know until we got there.*

My brother and I knew nothing of this incident until we found and read a transcript of the retirement ceremony after his death, when we also learnt that my father was renowned for recounting his war stories to friends and colleagues. He never told them at home.

The second trip I remember was very different. Early in 1945 we turned off the gas, electricity and water, locked the doors and decamped to Cadgwith Cove, a fishing village in Cornwall close to where my father was stationed at Predannack. Imagine being five years old, accustomed to a cramped cottage on the outskirts of a blacked-out, smoggy, industrial town and being transported to an airy bungalow in a seaside hamlet with a sunny climate. Not only were the surroundings new and exciting, but my father was also often about, together with his fellow airmen who brought us sweets and played with us. I became very attached to one of them and used to hang about the door hoping that he would arrive before I had to go to bed, though now I recall no more than his name, Redfern. I have an impression that he, like Herbert, died in action.

In Cornwall I enjoyed a room to myself at the end of a corridor. With the door open I fell asleep wrapped in the sound of voices, laughter and sometimes singing from the other side of the house, perhaps stirring later as a motorcycle roared off into the night. My father taught us snatches of the songs they sang. One was a squadron song, sung to the tune of *The Old Grey Mare*:

> *The 151, she ain't what she used to be,*
> *Ain't what she used to be,*

Ain't what she used to be.
The 151, she ain't what she used to be,
Ever since the WAAFs joined up.

and another, to the tune of *Lily Marlene*:

Come out of the hanger, out into the light,
Taxi down the runway and take-off in the night.
We leave the flare-path far behind,
It's dark up here, but we don't mind.
We're off to bomb Ben Ghazi,
We're off to bomb BGs.

In the mornings we ate breakfast in the airy kitchen with the resident seagull, Billy, perched on the windowsill raucously demanding his share. Then it was time for school. Though I cannot remember the school, which was in Ruan Minor, I had good reason to remember the journey to it. David and I walked there together; down the steep road overlooking the sea, along past the lifeboat house and up through a field where, all too often, grazed a massive, though supposedly docile, bull. Unconvinced of its docility we hurried along the winding path, David in determined silence and I clutching his hand and never taking my eyes off the beast. Apart from an occasional stare it ignored us, but the fear that walked with me on those morning journeys is my one unhappy memory of the period.

The return journey was no problem. My mother collected us as she always had, often taking us to paddle or play on the beach. Sometimes there were other children about, often two brothers called Drew who were Londoners, temporarily living at the Post Office and joined by their father at weekends. They were David's friends largely, being too old for me, so I often played on my own. The shingle beach, where my mother sometimes bought red mullet from the fishermen, lay in the shadow of the cliffs. At one end there was a nasty smell of fish and the dank seaweed harboured sand-flies that bit me, but I forgot them in the pleasures it provided. Pebbles scrunching under my feet, I clambered round the drawn-up fishing boats, helped David build towers of stones to knock down or just threw stones into the sea. Stacks of cane lobster-pots invited my poking fingers and I searched the salty heaps of ropes and nets for the green glass floats which fascinated me with their smoothness and secret insides.

The fishing beach was separated from an equally small sandy one by a rocky outcrop which was so low in the middle that at high tide the outer part became an island. It was an exciting place of rough rocks, sharp barnacles and salty pools teeming with tiny crabs and fish. David scrambled across it easily enough, but for me it was hard going, especially the bit in the middle. I followed him across it stubbornly, as ever wanting do what he did but also for the thrill of the deep, concealed pool that the receding tide left on top of it. In truth I was a bit frightened, so always responded readily to my mother's call: 'Joan, come on back. The tide's turned. David, don't stay too long. You'll get trapped.'

It was always Mother who watched over us on the beach. When my father was there he would soon swim out beyond the rocks before turning to float on his back in the blue, sunlit water. Sitting beside her, I sensed her unease as we watched his head appearing and disappearing in the waves, but now I can imagine how he must have relished those brief escapes from his war-filled world.

Sometimes, when my father had time off, we caught the bus to other places. We picnicked on different beaches at Mullion, Kynance and Kennack, with seemingly endless sand to dig and caves to explore, walked on the headland to watch the churning seas at the Lizard and even went to the RAF camp. David, at nine, was old enough to appreciate sitting in the cockpit of his father's Mosquito. Even later in life he could hardly believe that as a small boy he sat at the controls of a plane which might very well have been on a bombing raid that same night. I remember no more than being lifted into it. What pleased me was visiting the camp storeroom; going through a black door into one of a dull-looking row of nissen huts to find it lined with shelf upon shelf of the big shiny tins in which my father brought home extras like sugar and jam, and the barley sugars issued to aircrew.

There was talk of our staying in Cornwall, but it was not to be. The idyll abruptly ended. My maternal grandfather died and it was back to Blackburn to sort out his affairs. We left in such confusion that I left behind a penny I had hidden under a stone outside the lifeboat house one day rather than carry it to school, an omission which became a family joke. Years later, when my parents returned to Cadgwith on holiday, I received a postcard of the lifeboat house saying that the penny had gone.

What I did take home was my bed. In Blackburn I had been sleeping in a cot with the sides removed and I desperately wanted to keep the collapsible iron bedstead I used in Cornwall. Whether it travelled north or a replacement was substituted I shall never know, but I slept on it, or its twin, until David left home and our bedroom became mine, though special coupons had to be obtained for purchase of the bedding.

My grandad, a widower in my memory though he married twice and had five children, lived in a tobacconists and sweet shop at No. 123 Victoria Street. Family legend says that the grandmother who died before I was born was a teacher, the well-educated daughter of an Oldham foundry manager. Since my widowed grandfather was a mere employee, unacceptable as a suitor, the couple eloped, lived first in Ashton then moved to Blackburn and rented the shop from which my mother eventually escaped to an office job at Rushton Son & Kenyon. She enjoyed that, remaining until David's birth brought her working life to an end.

At one time Grandad also ran a second shop on Redlam and two huts from which he sold ice cream, one at Wilpshire and another at Copster Green, but it was the Victoria Street shop which played its part in my childhood. It was double-fronted, cool and shady in summer as goods obscured one window and the other had a solid back which kept the light out, but it was cold in winter as the door was normally open. Inside, backed by shelves crammed with tobacco, cigarettes and jars of sweets, were wooden counters topped by glass display cases which framed the serving areas. They held smoking paraphernalia such as pipes, spills and cigarette rolling devices, and a fascinating array of oddments including Fennings Little Healers. We children used those as marbles, rolling the pills around on the counter for a while before returning them to their boxes for sale. There was also a locked cabinet containing the herbal medicines which Grandad concocted in addition to making ice cream.

The ice cream churns were set into the counter, next to the flap which I enjoyed being small enough to walk under to reach the door to the living area at the back. Beside them stood stone jars of Duttons sarsaparilla, which I grew to like almost as much as the ice cream. I was not alone. There was usually a customer or two sitting on the bench along the third wall, eating ice cream with the bone spoons I still use, drinking sarsaparilla, smoking, or simply chatting to my grandad. Oddly, since I remember the shop so well with its mingled odours of tobacco and sweet stuff, the squeal of the blind being raised and the dankness of the living room, I hardly remember him at all.

Neither my mother nor her sister had any interest in keeping the shop after their father's death, partly because they had both been forced to help with the business as children. My mother served behind the counter in the morning before she went to school while Jessie, from the age of five, caught the first tram to Wilpshire with churns of ice cream for the huts. Later my mother was made to leave school to work in the shop, something which she resented and complained about for the rest of her life. 'Your father's not the only one with brains,' she insisted from time to time. 'I was clever at school but I had to leave and work in the shop as soon as I was 14, though Jessie didn't, just because she was younger. My teacher came to talk to my father about it, but it didn't make any difference.'

Other than that, she always spoke fondly of her father. He was a keen member of the Territorial Army, based at Canterbury Street Barracks, and when he went off to camp in Southport during the summer she and Jessie went too, staying with relatives nearby. Though the family finances were drained by medical costs for my ailing grandmother, as young women they had the time and money to go out and enjoy themselves. They smoked, went out dancing and were members of various clubs – my mother the Field Club and then the Rambling Club, Aunty Jessie the Cyclists' Touring Club, and both of them a swimming club. Aunty Jessie played the banjulele while my mother was sufficiently accomplished on the violin to perform in a concert in the Overlookers' Hall in 1927. It was only the curtailed education and having to work in the shop that upset her.

Even so, in the autumn of 1945, she and Aunty Jessie kept the business going as they tried to sell it, leaving me, David and Christine to run wild in the Victoria Street area as they did so. Let loose in an unfamiliar urban environment and assuming that no one knew who we were, we knocked on doors and ran away, chalked all over the pavements – for which we got into serious trouble from the house-proud householders whose brushed and swilled fronts we were defacing – sneaked in and out of the nearby shops, swung on their sun blinds and roamed the streets and backs. Younger and more timid than the others I was sometimes too frightened to enjoy these antics and hid in the dim cavern of Field's outfitters, or sneaked off to watch the clog-maker who lived a few of doors away from the shop. He made the red leather clogs I wore to school in winter, edged with shiny studs and fitted with irons which made bright sparks in the drab playground. Lingering in his doorway I savoured the smell of leather and newly shaved wood just as I did the cloying, damp odour of the nearby paper mill. The mill burnt down more than once in my childhood – for the insurance money according to my mother. It was built on the slope behind Gregson's butchers so that the sunny window sill I used to sit on was at ground level at one end while my feet dangled in the air at the other. I often lingered there while David and Christine climbed up to a roof overlooking the yard to watch the bales of rags being unwrapped and coal shovelled into the blazing furnace.

A sale was eventually agreed and the £300 it brought in was divided between the four surviving children: my mother, Aunty Jessie, their half sister, Florrie – who lived in Preston and whom I never met – and their half brother, Harry, from Manchester. I remember him, but only as impossible to talk to, being stone deaf as a result of driving gun carriage mules in World War One.

The business was bought by the Berry sisters, twins who lived round the corner in James Street, who ran the shop as a lock-up and used the rear of the premises for their existing wreath-making business. This fascinated me and I spent hours standing in the cool, glassed lean-to at the back, breathing in the soft scent of pine from the fronds they were using and admiring their deft finger-work as they swiftly twisted together the fine wires and foliage to create works of art. Apart from this, it shames me to admit that I remember them most for being so badly crippled by rickets that their legs formed lozenge shapes, giving them a strange gait and reducing their height so that they almost disappeared below the shop counters. I liked them, and my mother explained their sickness to me, but their physical appearance always made me feel uncomfortable.

My mother got on so well with the sisters that for many years we continued to call and buy our sweet ration and my father's tobacco from them. She also continued to shop in Victoria Street, mainly for bread, cakes and meat. Choosing my pudding from an array of fancy cakes – perhaps a savoy, a madeleine or a meringue – was a great treat, as was watching the butcher (who used to give me silky rabbits' tails for luck) churn out sausages from the machine which stood at the back of the window, half hidden by loops of black pudding and red-skinned polony.

Our fruit and vegetables came from the indoor market, fish from the fish market – which I walked through holding my nose – and almost everything else from Blackburn's grocers on Revidge, collected or delivered. One of my regular errands was to take the order to the shop, another to go to Lora's nearby, to buy Spillers Shapes or Bonio from her paraffin perfumed general store. I suppose she was really called Laura, but as I watched her angular figure shovel dusty dog biscuits from hessian sack to paper bag, flowered overall protecting her dress, curlers descending from her headscarf turban, I failed to relate her name to that of the glamorous girls of my story books and simplified it in my head. I was also sent to the chip shop, which I did not enjoy since it was further away, the old newspapers I had to take were heavy, and there was always a lengthy wait. However many times I went, while the basin I handed over was warmed, filled with my order and wrapped in insulating newspaper, I found myself relieving the tedium by mentally completing the blanks in the Tizer advert on the wall behind the counter, though I had known the answers for years.

Though the brief period of rampaging around Victoria Street ended with the sale of the business, I hardly missed it. My immediate environment had everything I could have wished for as a playground: overgrown shrubbery laced by secret paths, overhanging bushes forming ready-made dens, trees and walls to climb, tarmac areas for ball games and, when it rained, plenty of room under the shed. There were also some once elegant greenhouses, then damp, decaying and virtually disused, which I liked to sneak into.

I can see myself now, furtively turning the knob and slowly pushing open the narrow door, aware of transgressing, thrilled by it. I step onto the ornate iron grills which floor the walkway, covering the rusting pipes and drainage channel below. However gently I tread, the loose metal sections clang beneath my feet as I move through to the next house and the next, relishing the pungent smell of earth and damp vegetation, enjoying the sense of a separate world. I peer into the water tank, stir the green surface scum with a twig and look for movement. Suddenly I hear a squeal, but not of an animal – a wheelbarrow. The gardener!

Fear grips me and I'm out of the door, through the neglected raspberry canes, down the slippery path which joins drive to drive, round the corner and under the shed to safety. The squeal represented our wealthy neighbours; the occupants of the big house, owners of all this glorious wilderness – and our cottage – and not entirely child tolerant.

Whinfield House was built in 1879 at a time when Blackburn's wealthy businessmen were moving into mansions to the west of the town, clear of industrial grime but close enough to attend to their affairs. It seemed like a palace to me with not one but two imposing entrances, each reached by a flight of steps. It was set parallel to the main road with lawns descending steeply from the drive in front of it to a hedged and therefore concealed path. Beyond that, a shrub border fronted the boundary wall on Preston New Road. The lower lawn, out of sight of the house, was tremendous for rolling down. The gardener, who was ancient (otherwise he would have been more usefully employed or at war) managed to keep this front area tended, in addition to growing some vegetables in the smallest of the three greenhouses. While other large houses and gardens were falling into disrepair all around us, Whinfield remained occupied throughout my childhood, although always divided into two. One half was home to a widow and her grown-up son, together with their housekeeper, with whom my mother became good friends; the other belonged to our landlord. He never bothered us, in fact he gave me and David shillings at Christmas, for which we were very grateful, but his wife was a different matter. She was the chief ogre of my childhood.

Quite why Old Witchy, as we called her, objected so strongly to our endless games of hide and seek or cowboys and indians in her acres of overgrown woods and shrubbery was never clear to me. We did no damage, but object she certainly did, even to the extent of chasing us. This made for even better games with real excitement, never dulled by the knowledge that she had not much chance of catching us. It particularly suited me since it meant we were all on the same side for a while. As next to the youngest of our little group, and often the only girl, I was always liable to be captured and lashed to the copper beech tree near the top of the drive. I liked Mondays when the washing line was not available.

Only once did Old Witchy come anywhere near catching anyone. She spotted us crossing the drive into the plot, the old tennis court my father turned into a vegetable patch after his demob, and hobbled up towards us, shouting angrily. The others were fast enough to escape but I was forced to take cover in a rhododendron, alone for once and very close to her. I could hear her mutterings, her footsteps, and then her laboured breathing as she stopped beside my bush. I crouched low to the ground, holding my breath, watching the hem of her long coat, the thick lisle stockings and heavy brogues. My senses heightened, the smell of earth suddenly seemed very strong and I could feel the damp on my bare knees.

'Come out of there. Come on out. I know where you are. I can see you.' I peered up through the waxy, green leaves, moving only my eyes. No she couldn't. She was looking the other way. I relaxed, but then she moved closer, her back even more hunched than usual as she peered towards me and began to thrash at the branches with one of her sticks. I was trembling now. Would she hit me? Was I finally going to be caught? I certainly would be if I tried to run. Where was my brother? Would he save me? I screwed up my eyes, crossed my fingers and tried not to breathe. I was small, the rhododendron big and thick, so she passed me by as she struggled further and further into the shrubbery, driven by disproportionate fury. I slipped out into the drive where we reassembled behind her, stifling our relieved laughter as we made for home.

Did she complain to my mother? Were we unconsciously adding to her wartime burdens with our innocent games? We must have been, but I never knew it, although I did know that my mother had no more time for her landlady than we had. Even in those stringent times the couple employed a housemaid – to my mind as cantankerous as her mistress – as well as the gardener, but when our house needed repair or maintenance she would come stumping across to inspect and declare everything an unnecessary expense. Then it was back to discussion with the rent man, who came for the money every Friday night. Eventually some of the work might be done, but more than the wrangling and frustration, I think it was having to submit to the arrogant behaviour and patronising attitude – the implication that we were not good enough to merit a decent house – which really upset my mother. The pressures of wartime, which were just life to me, made her ill. In later years I caught references to a nervous breakdown, a state which I suppose would now be diagnosed as stress or depression and treated, but I never learnt much about her suffering. In an era where mental illness was seen as shameful and something to be concealed, she concealed it.

By the time my father returned to us permanently, sporting the brown demob suit that was to be his only decent outfit for a long time, I had been out of the Babies and in a proper classroom for over a year. During that time David, since he had taken me to school in Cornwall, had become my escort to St Silas', and not always a patient one. He sometimes deserted me and, quite early in this arrangement, his impatience precipitated a step in my growing up. I was devoted to my teddy bear, so much so that I could not sleep without him, and it was a long time before I forgave my brother when he cut the fur off his tummy. On this occasion I had insisted on taking Teddy to school, but by the time we reached the top of the lane I was already tired of carrying him. 'David, will you carry Teddy?' I whined.

'No. You wanted to bring him. You carry him.'

'I can't. I'm going to take him home.'

'No you're not. There isn't time.' I stood there, mutinously, Teddy dangling from one hand.

'Oh, come on! Throw him over the wall. I'll collect him on the way back.'

'But he might not be there.'

'Well make your mind up. I'm not carrying a stupid bear. We're going to be late. I'm going.' I was left snivelling in the deserted lane. Almost as angry with my beloved bear as I was with David, I instinctively drew back my arm to throw him away, but paused, and thought. I saw for myself the truth of my mother's repeated warnings: 'If you do that you'll be sorry.' I lingered, debated with myself, then reluctantly lugged Teddy to school – and I still have him.

In school, rows of desks had replaced miniature tables and chairs, slates now came in green with wooden frames and I had a blackboard and easel to focus on. I remember the blackboard distinctly, not because of its instructional value but because it fell on a classmate's head and knocked her out. There were no serious consequences, but when she was carried away I thought she was dead and was surprised to see her the following week.

I suppose I remember the slates for the wrong reason too. The playing years were done with as the fair but fierce Miss Lister descended on us with the three Rs. Thanks to my mother I was well ahead in two of them, but less proficient in arithmetic, so I was glad I could rub out my mistakes with a licked finger, one of the few advantages of the paper shortage. Next came the gentler but equally strict Miss Lupton, head of the infants, preparing us for the rigours of the Junior School upstairs. By this time we had specific morning and afternoon playtime: 10 or 15-minute breaks when we were turned out of the building unless it was raining really hard, just as we were at dinner time. From five years old that was the only playing we did in school time, boys in one yard, girls in the other, and woe betide anyone who passed through the door in the wall which separated them. Talking to a brother or sister was no excuse. Thus the football and cricket I was used to at home were denied me. Instead I spent my time vainly trying to do handstands and cartwheels on the tarmac, joining in singing games and playing two-ball interminably against the school wall in addition to the common, seasonal activities.

One of my favourites of the seasonal games was conkers, since I frequently did well. After all, I had the pick of the crop from the horse chestnut trees by the house and along Meins Road. Some of my schoolfellows, the Nightingales, Shorrocks and Lucases, lived in farms at the far end of it, but most of them lived in the steep, treeless streets near school. Even in the years I had a poor score I enjoyed gathering the gleaming chestnut kernels and searching out the biggest to string and dry for battle, though at first David bored the holes for me. Conkers, of course, was an autumn activity. What order the rest came in, or what prompted the changes, was never obvious to me. Skipping with long ropes came in summer – I remember red Clark's sandals and summer dresses as I queued to run through or jump over the rope, nervously because I was not very good at it – but bowling hoops, yo-yo, singing games, whip and top and the rest could have been at any time. Whip and top was another favourite, nothing less on my whip than a leather thong acquired from the clog maker near the shop. Not only did it make the top spin long and true, the coloured whorls running and shifting like silk, but I could crack the whip in the air and lash the top with a satisfying swish.

In winter there were some advantages in the separation of the sexes at playtime. Until four o'clock we girls were safe from vicious snowball attacks, from having our snowmen destroyed or being ousted by boys from the slides we made. Girls, however, could be ousted from slides by girls, and I frequently was. It was even worse than being the last one when teams were picked and, try as I would, I could do nothing about it. It was not that I fell over, pushed out of turn or slid more slowly than anyone else; those were acceptable crimes. My crime was to slide with my left foot forward, when everyone else used the right. As a result, when the air filled with the squeals and shrieks of joyful children, I would often be huddled against the wall, rejected as a destroyer of slides. I have some early memories of that playground in summer, but mostly it is winter. I feel the misery of isolation, stare at the crates of frozen milk stacked against the toilet block and wait for the whistle that will release me.

Despite our squabbles en route and ignoring each other during the day, when David left St Silas' I missed him. Though I was small for my age, life with a big brother whose regular tormenting had taught me to fight and stand up for myself meant I was in little danger of being bullied at school, but he was still my protector. Though not normally a fighter, when he heard someone at school had hit me he quietly sought him out and beat him up, and that was the end of that. I was soon to learn that his presence had also protected me closer to home.

At sometime he and I had found a length of thick rope on Preston New Road, the kind used to lash loads onto lorries. One evening, as I played with it in the lane after school, a classmate I disliked because he had started chasing me and lifting my skirt up on the way home once David was at secondary school, ran off with it. I was ridiculously attached to that piece of rope and rushed into the house sobbing.

'What on earth's the matter?' my mother asked, seeing no sign of scrapes or bruises.

'Edward's stolen the rope,' I eventually gulped out. 'He chased me and stole it.' I said nothing about the skirt lifting. I had no idea why he did it but it made me feel ashamed, so I kept quiet. My mother was incensed. It was still a time when we had few toys and the boy was from a wealthy family, one of the sort she was inclined to resent because it seemed to her that their men folk had not gone to war but stayed at home and made money out of it. At her lowest ebb even Uncle Billy, who had a reserved occupation as a toolmaker at Northrop, sank into this category.

Together we set off towards Edward's house, looking over walls and through gateways as we went, but without success. Eventually, since my mother always nerved herself in defence of her children, I found myself clutching her hand as we climbed the steep garden path leading to their front steps. I wanted my rope, but was frightened at the thought of trouble and felt slightly sick as she rang the bell. It was opened by a well-dressed lady with an unwelcoming face.

'Yes?' she inquired, staring down at us in a way that made me feel even worse. My mother explained. 'I'll ask him,' she conceded, and left us on the doorstep. She was away for no more than a moment. 'Edward,' she declared haughtily, 'has no rope,' and closed the door in our faces. So we lost the rope, but at least he left me alone after that, even taking a different route home.

But I missed David's company as well as his protection. Our adored dog was now my only companion up and down the lane every day. Met with our longing for a pet, one of the first things my father did following his demob was to take us to the police station on Northgate to get a dog. There we were led to the dog pound in the bowels of the building to be faced with rows of cages containing lost or abandoned animals. The commotion when we arrived was horrible. There were all sorts and sizes of dogs, whining, barking, and scrabbling at the wire. I knew they were destined to be destroyed and wanted to save them all. We walked up and down for ages, looking at the frantic animals and stroking the noses poking through the bars. It was hard, but eventually we made our choice and escaped with a squirming, black puppy with a white front, gleaming fur, silky ears and an appealing face. He pranced about the pavements outside as we went to buy his licence, but disliked the top deck of the bus, where all dogs and smokers had to travel. He huddled in the front corner below the notice prohibiting spitting, quivering and whimpering, until my father picked him up and we could all stroke him. We called him Peter – I have no idea why – and though he barked a lot at strangers who came near the house and sometimes frightened people in the lane, he was a very gentle dog. If I was alone and upset, he would sit patiently with an occasional sympathetic whimper as I hugged him and shed my tears into his soft fur. He was also obedient and well-behaved. Mother saw to that.

Now there was only me to send him home from the top of the lane every morning and pet him when I found him waiting there on my return. He knew when it was time for school to end and scratched at the door until my mother opened it. In addition he was always let out when anyone was expected home after dark and appeared at the main gate to be an escort through the shadow-black, shrubbery lined drive.

Dangerous Diversions

David soon began to lead me astray outside Whinfield Place as well as in it. The first occasion I remember, not too long after my father's return, might well have been a disaster without the intervention of the same Haydocks with whom he had left his wartime message for my mother. We lived very close to the main house, in its outbuildings effectively, about 200 yards away from the main entrance to the grounds on Preston New Road. There was a lodge just inside the gates, beyond which the drive forked. Left led to a turning circle in front of the mansion and then round it to the shed where we lived, while right went up the hill and past the derelict tennis court of my near capture by Old Witchy. Beyond that it was bordered by five modern houses, in one of which the writer Dorothy Whipple later lived, before reaching another gate leading into the lane opposite the nursery where our rhubarb and tomatoes came from. The neighbours here, beyond the path which ran across the top of our garden, were above us both geographically and in income. Mother would never have presumed on their acquaintance, though my father had no such qualms, but they were friendly and sometimes figured in our lives.

David had a friend, Michael I think it was, who lived on a smallholding at Mellor Brook. He invited us to stay with him, tempting us with the prospect of collecting eggs, feeding goats, picking fruit and generally messing about but our parents, who had not met the family, would not allow it. There was no point in arguing – 'No!' always meant just that, and any protest a row – but David was determined to go. He told Michael we would, and one lovely summer morning, carrying some clothes and the contents of our moneyboxes, we went.

We had two moneyboxes each by then. One, in the shape of a metal book, was for savings to be added to the Yorkshire Penny Bank accounts we had started through school at a penny a week. That had to be taken to the bank in Lord Street West to be unlocked. The other was for spending money, and could be opened with a screwdriver – or the potato peeler. David's was a metal fort, mine a brightly clad black man, though not the superior model Christine had with a moving hand which fed the coins into his mouth. These David emptied the day before.

How he woke himself in the morning I do not know. I imagine he left the plywood blackout cover open so that the dawn light shone through the skylight, but he certainly had to waken me. 'Come on,' he was whispering urgently as I struggled to open my eyes. 'They'll waken up soon, and anyway we have to catch the bus.'

The door squealed as we left the room and the dog stirred at the bottom of the stairs. We paused, watching the partly open door of our parents' room. A slight movement but nothing more, so on down the stairs, keeping close to the banisters to stop the treads creaking. Safely into the kitchen, the bolts drawn back, and we were away. 'Run,' David commanded, and we fled as far as the deserted A577 and crossed to the bus stop just on the Preston side of the gate. We were used to catching the Ribble bus there. When my father was first demobbed he returned to his job as a debt collector for a finance company in Preston, and in the school holidays my mother sometimes took us there to play by the river before going to meet him.

It seemed to me that we stood at the stop for a long time as the day warmed up around us with only the sound of the birds for company. Just as the bus appeared, Mr Haydock walked across and joined us. We climbed on, going inside for once rather than upstairs as David was not too sure where to get off, and he followed and sat behind us.

'Hello Joan, David. You're out early. Where are you off to?'

'We're going to see David's friend. He lives on a farm and there'll be animals and things, and we're going to have bacon and eggs for breakfast.'

'Whereabouts is that?'

'Well, it's not really a farm,' explained my brother, from the height of his 10 years. 'It's just a small holding and Michael's dad goes out to work as well. You get off the bus just past the junction and it's down a track on the left-hand side. This is it, here. Bye Mr Haydock. Come on, Joan. Hurry up!'

Out in the soft morning air again we paused before heading between thick hedges towards a red roof David could just see above them. Michael and his mother greeted us with what she imagined was our second breakfast, which we ate in the kitchen. I found that strange, since our own kitchen was barely big enough for two people to stand in, let alone sit down, and our only flat surface the enamelled top of the folded down mangle, crammed against the stone sink. As David chattered away I sat in shy silence, marvelling at the big stove and the walls of cupboards. Our cooker was flanked by shelves made by my father from orange boxes scrounged from the grocer to supplement the one proper cupboard which held our pots. Tinned food and dry goods were stored in the windowless larder under the stairs with perishables in a mesh-fronted food safe, with a mouse trap underneath it for the times we had no cat. I would have been quite happy for any mouse, or the cat, to devour the government issue cod-liver oil which was also kept in there. We were dosed with it daily and I loathed the stuff. Fortunately we were also provided with Haliborange, which more or less took the taste away.

We soon moved outside with an impatient Michael, but our adventure was to be very short-lived. The Haydocks had a phone and within a very short time Mrs Haydock was knocking on our door asking if our parents knew where we were. Oddly, my clearest memory is not of my mother's arrival and our ignominious return home on the next bus, but of our hostess's horror at discovering that she had been entertaining two runaways. I escaped with a telling-off, being deemed too young to be responsible, but David was given a thrashing when my father returned from work. He was now the final authority in the household. Mother's wartime threat, 'Behave, or I'll bring a policeman,' had become 'Behave, or I'll tell your father.'

Now it was always Mother, too, never Ma or Mum or Mummy. The first time my father heard my brother address my mother as Mummy he took us into town and marched us into the museum, a silent, gloomy place with equally silent and gloomy exhibits displayed in heavy glass cases. Once inside he led us through room after room, voices hushed but footsteps pattering on the heavy linoleum, until we reached the Egyptian section. Here he pointed to a long, thin object swathed in dirty bandages. 'That,' he said, 'is a mummy,' and we listened dutifully while he told us all about it. 'So don't let me hear you use that word to your mother again,' he concluded. We didn't. We had learnt not to argue, and in this case we'd seen his point. He remained Daddy though, until, as we grew older, they slipped unremarked into Mum and Dad.

Quite apart from this salutary experience, I never liked the main museum. The alternative, the Lewis Textile Museum, was more to my taste with its life-sized models in period costume gazing vacantly at me from the glass rooms in which they were entombed with their early looms and spinning machines. They were colourful and had some connection with my known world – and the labels were not written in faded black ink on curling yellow paper. It was also comfortably small, though not my favourite space in the collection of public buildings beside the Town Hall. That was the Art Gallery. It was light and airy, untainted by the all-consuming brown of the museum beside it, and its silence was peaceful rather than intimidating. I would like to claim I developed a love of art at an early age but no, it was just a love of the long polished benches and the curving banisters on the staircase, which seemed to have been designed for children to slide on.

Even better for sliding, though of a different kind, was the ice of the terrible winter of 1947, David's final year at St Silas' and my first in the Junior School. The weather was so bad that many pupils never arrived, playtimes were cancelled and the school occasionally closed because of the shortage of coke for the boiler. That, however, made no difference to the behaviour of Miss Middleton, better known to us as Miggy, then David's teacher. Outwardly she was a paragon of virtue: choir mistress, pillar of the church and a very successful teacher. Indeed she was all these things, but in many of her pupils' eyes she was cruel and unsympathetic, ruling by fear and never to be forgotten. Unusually she ran a car, a small convertible ATJ 906, and its very appearance cleared the street of children. Years later I heard Russell Harty describing the harshness of one of his former teachers in a radio interview. I missed the name but had no doubt it was Miggy. Russell went to St Silas' too.

One day that memorable winter David, already one of Miggy's targets for refusing to join the church choir despite having a beautiful singing voice, forgot to put his tie on before he rushed out to school. Miggy refused to have him in the classroom and sent him home through a blizzard to get it, forcing him to struggle back up Woodbine Road through snowdrifts that we had discovered on the way there were deeper than I was tall. Mother kept him at home and, when she came to collect me, driven by her anger found the courage to complain.

But for us that winter was fun; jumping in and out of drifts, slithering and sliding everywhere, pushing and tumbling. We also rolled enormous snowballs and built an igloo outside our back window big enough to crawl inside. David, Christine and I made snowballs which he and my father then built into a dome while she and I filled the gaps with loose snow. It lasted for weeks. Walking on the duck pond in Corporation Park was another novelty, as was watching skaters on Queen's Park lake, where my mother had skated as a child. We also sledged until we were almost tired of it.

We owned a splendid sledge, a wooden one, painted dark green, with a seat big enough for two, metal runners and a crossbar that made it easy to go down head first. It must have been inherited or second or third hand; there would have been no money to buy such a thing. We needed to go no further than the lane where David would whiz down from the steep part by the house to crunch to a halt on the cinders my father spread at the bottom to stop us running into Preston New Road. There was no danger of my doing that; I only ever started from halfway down. Sometimes, though, we went to join the crowds on Spying Cop – not until a recent visit to South Africa did it occur to me that it was Spion Kop, named after the Boer War battle site – at the West Leigh Road end of the golf course. That was altogether different: an unobstructed run in cushioning snow, underlain by grass not stones, which saw even me hurtling down, steering wildly, thrilling to the speed and screaming and shouting with the rest. I was not so enthusiastic when it came to dragging the sledge back home. When my father was there he dragged me on it. David would not.

Though we now had a father who was present, who entertained us and took us out, David and I still spent much of our time close to home where he continued to lead me into mischief, and sometimes danger. We climbed anything and everything, including the front garden wall beside the lane which had flat coping stones about 18 inches wide. There was a small, wooden gate in the angle formed by it and the lower boundary wall, so it was up the gate on to the first wall, up a rose trellis and onto the top. There I perched, unnoticed, watching people in the lane some 12ft below or just enjoying the different perspective of my surroundings.

One day I found the courage to follow my brother and cousin along the wall to touch the house, so doubling the drop and bringing me almost to gutter level.

I was content to make it and turning to go back when David climbed from the wall onto the gutter and began to move along it away from me, Christine close behind him. About 6ft away a gully sloped up by the chimney breast. In no time at all they were up that, over the edge of the flat area of the roof and out of sight. As ever, I followed.

Toes on the gutter, I spread-eagled myself against the sloping slates and tentatively edged my way along. When I finally reached the chimney I was stranded. I was too small to reach the roof to pull myself up and too scared to stand up and walk without handholds in the brickwork beside me. 'David!' I shouted. 'David, I'm stuck.' His startled face appeared over the edge of the roof.

'Go back! You shouldn't have come.'

'Come down and help me.'

'I can't. You're in the way.' I looked at him, looked back the way I had come and stayed put, silenced by fear. Finally he leant down, managed to reach my hands and dragged me up beside him to sit for a while on the warm lead. Soon, fear forgotten, I too was walking about, stepping carefully over the raised strips which broke up the grey surface. It felt strange up there, on top of our house and next door, almost level with some of the tree tops. The area I stood on sloped into space all around me. I felt excited, free. But I still had to get down. David went first, helping me slide down the gully to join him then encouraging my progress back along the gutter. My parents remained ignorant of that exploit but my father spotted, and put an end to, something potentially as dangerous.

David had been reading escape stories and decided we should build a tunnel. The obvious place for this was the old tennis court area, where he selected a spot very close to the rhododendron bushes in which I had hidden from Old Witchy. She no longer bothered us, perhaps because my father was back. The three of us, for Christine was part of this escapade too, began to dig. It was during the holidays so we were able to dig for the best part of a week, using the gardening tools from the coal shed and fashioning pit props from fallen branches. We succeeded in making a tunnel big enough for two of us to crawl inside at the same time and started to build the sloping exit, but the weekend put an end to it. My father came to tend his vegetables, became suspicious of our silence in the shrubbery and came to find us. Horrified, he removed the props and stamped all over the ground until the tunnel roof collapsed.

'You idiots,' he stormed. 'You could all have suffocated. David, you're old enough to have more sense. Did you want to kill your sister and your cousin as well as yourself? All of you, pick up those spades, fill in this hole and come and fetch me when you've done it.' Though we were both confined to the house for the rest of the day, once again I escaped with a telling off while David was thrashed. Christine was sent home to be punished by her parents when she had to explain her early return. The Gills, who would once have been fellow culprits, no longer played any part in our activities. They had left and the house next door was empty, leaving us with no more than the occasional company of three nephews of other neighbours who came to stay during the holidays. Two of them were nearer David's age and reluctant to include me in their activities. The third, George, was younger. I remember him particularly for startling me with a proud demonstration of how far he could project his wee. 'I bet I can hit that rock from here,' he said, apropos of nothing, and started to unfasten his shorts. He did hit it. A house now stands on the spot.

He and I were much of an age and played together happily until the summer one of his boarding school friends came to stay. He refused to play cricket if I played and jeered at George for playing with a girl at all. As a result he never played with me again. I was hurt, but accepted it. After all, as far as I could see, girls nearly always came second to boys in what they were allowed to do and in the fuss made of them. That was partly why I wanted to be a boy.

With my father's presence, my world quickly expanded beyond Whinfield's walls. Before the war my parents had been fond of walking. Indeed they met in the Rambling Club, or more properly Blackburn Rambling Association, not an affiliated group of the national association but an independent club of which they were founder members. They were delighted to be awarded life membership for their Golden Wedding, and the bench that the club erected in my father's memory is now a landmark on the town's Tacklers Trail. Not only did he walk all his life, but my father also took an active interest in footpath preservation. As early as 1940, three months after my birth, he spoke at a rally in Downham.

After his demob my parents soon returned to walking and the club, naturally taking me and David with them. The walks were usually around Blackburn, using buses to get to the start once we had gathered on the Boulevard by Queen Victoria's Statue – the universal meeting place. Rain or shine saw us tramping the moors and fields and calling at farms and cottages for jugs of tea to share as we ate the food we carried with us, sometimes in the houses or outbuildings, but more often outside. One of the cottages, on Whalley Nab, I always looked forward to because of the swing in the garden, another, in Mellor, I remember for its two-seater, wooden box lavatory set over a stream. Almost all the places we called at had outside privies, mostly with torn squares of newspaper hanging on a nail for toilet paper, just as my grandad and some of my friends had, but they were not like these country ones in that they were whitewashed and had chains to pull. Many of the rural ones, housed in rotting wooden sheds, did not flush at all but opened onto a stream or had a bucket under the hole and were so dirty, fly-infested and disgustingly smelly that I had to be desperate to use them.

David soon started grumbling at having to go on the walks at all, but I enjoyed them. I liked being out, seeing different places and people and learning about them from my parents and their friends as we tramped the countryside. It was from them that I learnt to distinguish oats from barley, spot a kestrel, identify a hazel tree and a host of other natural features; they fed my imagination with tales of the Lancashire Witches as we walked through Barley and Sabden, and it was because of them that I could recognise a Celtic cross or a packhorse bridge and visualise a countryside peopled with pedlars and travelling monks.

Often, in winter, we were overtaken by darkness at the end of rambles, so one of my early Christmas presents was a torch – a blue, plastic dog with a bulb in its mouth which fitted neatly into my pocket – but I did not always use it. Sometimes I preferred to be part of the shadowy world I was traversing rather than focusing on a tiny ellipse of light, especially in eerie stretches like the road from Downham to the bus stop in Chatburn, where we often finished up. Everyone was tired by then, so there was not much chatter, just the sound of footsteps with rarely so much as a single car to break the spell and blind me briefly before leaving a deeper blackness. It excited me to walk a few paces apart from the others, in the shadowy dimness of stars or a young moon, the bulk of Pendle Hill rising against the sky on my left, tree branches arching above to deepen the darkness at my feet, and somewhere an owl hooting. On cold, clear nights, however, if the moon was full, the thrill turned to fear and I stayed close within the group.

I remember parts of walks like that one, including lunch with paddling at Swanside Beck or climbing Darwen Tower, but no particular local walks or destinations. However, once a year the club went further afield, and one of those outings I do remember. I was seven years old and going to walk across Morecambe Bay for the first time.

We set out from Hest Bank, emerging from the train which stopped close to the shore, into bright, morning sunshine. We had risen early to get there, but I was too excited to feel tired and chased about on the beach with David and the dog, all of us glad to be out of the stuffy carriage. We were soon called back to join the circle which was forming round the guide, but I was not listening to what he was saying. I was looking at the sand, stretching out to the horizon, shimmering wetly in the distance. Was that really where we were going, I wondered. It looked so far, and so flat. All I could see ahead was sky.

My doubts were soon resolved. Shoes, socks and stockings were removed and put into bags or rucksacks to join the sandwiches, spare clothes, sou'westers and plastic macs already there. Men wearing long trousers rolled them up, we children were checked, and we were off. Like me, and of course David who was only 11 so not into long trousers, my father was wearing shorts as he always did for walking, even well into winter. My mother was clad in her customary old skirt. I never saw her wear anything else, though before she was married she used to walk in the brown corduroy shorts I inherited, which she changed into once she was out of her father's sight.

My father joined the guide at the front, maintaining his usual long, easy stride, and at first I padded alongside, holding his hand to help me cope with the soft dry sand, and this time listening as they talked about changing channels, the way the route was marked and how people used to make the crossing in stage coaches, sometimes setting out and never being seen again. I loved the stories, but when they began to talk about ordinary things, I left them.

By then we were walking on damper, softer sand, so I went to join my brother and the older children who were making lines of footprints, destroying worm casts and splashing through the shallow pools as they went along. David found a crab and chased me with it, and as I ran I could feel the cool, gritty particles forcing themselves up between my toes. Next we trod on the spot to make the ground quiver like jelly, and almost before I realised it, we were well out in the bay, and I could see the other side.

By this time we had crossed our first river channel, run through it in fact with a splendid splashing. I got really soaked when the dog followed and shook himself over me at the other side. It was glorious fun and I could taste salt all the time after that. It was several miles before I noticed that the shore ahead still looked a long way off, and dropped back to find my mother.

Just as my father always walked at the front on club rambles, so my mother always walked at the back, to his perpetual irritation. 'Come on Doris', he chided, after almost every rest, 'Start off at the front and then you won't be trailing.' It made no difference. She carried on walking at the back, chatting to her friends, as she was doing when I found her. She broke off her conversation to point out the salmon nets in the channel, and Grange baths which we were heading for and could now see quite clearly, but I was more interested in knowing how long it would take to get there. Wading through the deeper channels, paddling through surface water and across fine, smooth sand had been fine, but there had also been long stretches where the sand lay in hard, rippled ridges. I was tired and my feet were sore.

Eventually I could see that there was one final water channel between us and the Esplanade. By this time I had tired of charging across the water courses and when I got close I saw that even if I wanted to, it would be impossible. It was the main river channel and too deep, with water so cloudy with sediment that the bottom was invisible. Even the leaders of the group had paused on its banks. I could hear them talking as I arrived.

'Wasn't expecting this. I'll be wetting my trousers here.' Someone laughed.

'How deep, d'you reckon?'

'Tide's turned. Look at t'flow.'

'We can't stay here, and anyway, we'll soon dry in the sun.'

Then the guide's voice, 'No matter. We're a bit later than we might have been, but it's still quite safe. There's no quicksand, no strong current and it's not too deep yet.'

People began to wade in and I watched as David and my father crossed and turned to wave from the far bank. Then it was my turn. I stepped in cautiously, holding on to my mother who had hitched her skirt up high. David had been fine, being much taller than me as well as bolder, but I began to feel nervous as the cold, flowing water, which was pulling the sand from under my feet, climbed higher and higher towards my waist, and clung to her. 'Vic!' she called, 'Come and help.'

Back my father came, so I made the final crossing on his shoulders and soon we were all safely ashore – well not quite. Peter was still on the far side of the channel with the stragglers, running up and down the bank, putting his front paws into the water then backing off and trying somewhere else, alternately barking and whining as he did so. Calling and whistling did no good; my father had to go back again, pull him into the water and hold on to his collar as he swam across. Then we were free to sit on the rocks to eat our sandwiches before watching the tide obliterate our route as we walked along the seafront to Grange railway station to begin the long journey home.

As well as walking with the Rambling Club, we also walked as a family in our own area so that David and I were soon as familiar with the paths and lanes around Whinfield Place as we were with the grounds themselves. We regularly walked to and around Pleasington, Houghton Bottoms, Salmesbury Bottoms and Mellor, all villages within a range of about three miles to the west of our home, so that before long the closer places in between, together with the golf links, the park and the quiet streets to the east of our home, became our wider playground.

Billinge Wood was one area we frequented. It was private property, a part of the Witton Estate, but since the top of the hill it covered had been used as an observation post during the war it had become less protected. It was easily accessible from the track to the Yellow Hills, so named for their covering of gorse, which ran up beside it. My father took us there in the first place, looking at what remained of the military installations which he had frequented as an ARP warden. We invaded it on our own as much for the thrill of being where we thought we really should not be as for the place itself, but I also enjoyed the deserted tracks through it, silent and soft underfoot, tunnels of security when the wind wailed in the treetops. It was a magnified and awesome version of the familiar trees and shrubbery I delighted in closer to home. There were owls in the wood too. We heard them hooting as we lay in bed at night and one day spotted one in a hole in a tree by the boundary wall. I looked for it ever after, but never saw it again.

The Yellow Hills, one of the areas where Mitchell and Kenyon are believed to have faked their film reports of the Boer War, offered a different environment in being open ground, but their real attraction was two disused quarries. The top one, a fairly shallow depression on the summit of the hill with a small pool at the bottom, was a popular picnic spot in summer. It was fun clambering around the sides, searching for minnows, paddling or building paths across the water with flat stones. As we began to have more toys we took our model boats up there. I had a six inch wind-up motor boat which usually cruised in the bath, David a yacht about a foot long which he could just about push all the way across. It was a good place to fly the kites we made as well, or try to. Lovingly constructed to my father's design on wooden cross frameworks with paper glued on and tails made from plaited paper strips, they hardly ever worked. Windmills on sticks were about our limit. My father's talents were intellectual rather than practical. Uncle Frank did or helped with many of the DIY jobs in our house, ranging from re-covering the card table to the construction of David's fort and my dolls' house.

The second quarry was very different. Though still small it was a proper quarry, cut into the hill so making a cliff at the back. Its steep sides enclosed a wide pool, almost always in shade. The dark water made me shudder but on summer days it invited bathers. It was deep – deep enough to jump into and swim below the cliff, but few did so. Everyone knew a child had drowned there. We were forbidden to go near it without my parents. Even David more or less obeyed the injunction, though not until my father had caught him pushing a plank out onto the water and trying to balance on it, and read him the riot act. He went close, but never played in the water again. I was both fascinated and repelled, always pausing to stare from a distance as we passed but sufficiently scared not to be tempted, and to be frightened for my brother. The day we discovered the real swimming pool was more my kind of adventure.

I could feel the sun through my dress as I dawdled down the lane: not the part that passed our house but the lower section on the far side of Preston New Road. I was close to the gate into Troy where the granite sets which once provided carriage horses with a better footing and were now catching my sandals, gave way to stony earth. Uneasily I slashed at the nettles with the cane in my hand, visualising the neat rows of vegetables on the other side of the wall. Not long before, David had persuaded me to eat some of the succulent young peas planted there. My pleasure in the taste had been spoilt by my awareness that taking someone's carefully grown food was stealing and wrong, quite different from scrumping apples from the overhanging tree in the backyard up the hill behind me as we regularly did. I still felt ashamed and hurried past the blank gates, pausing beyond them to pluck a frond of grass from the summer hedgerow so I could chew on its juicy stem as I wandered on.

The lane became hotter, more enclosed, the hum of insects more intense. David and Christine were out of sight but I was not bothered; I knew the way. The cane

I held had a piece of string attached to it with a bent pin on the end, my brother was carrying a jam jar with more string knotted to form a handle and my cousin had some bits of bread in her pocket. We were going fishing close to the entrance to Billinge Scar.

Remembering it would be cool and shady by the stream, I began to walk a little more purposefully. I reached the open gateway, turned left between the railings and the wall and stopped. This was the place, but the others were nowhere to be seen. Hiding from me I supposed. Nothing unusual in that, but where? The woodland was too thin, the undergrowth too sparse. I decided they must be in the grounds of the house, retraced my steps to the entrance and listened. The quiet was disturbing. I could hear the distant trickle of the stream, a twittering bird, the buzz of an insect by my face, but no voices or movement. Hesitantly I stepped between the gateposts and listened again. Too nervous to walk up the drive I took to the shrubbery by the wall. Immediately I found the jam jar and David's cane. Reassured, I put mine down too, carried on and soon heard their whispers. They had forgotten all about me and were lying at the edge of the bushes, staring at the remains of a house. Glassless windows stared back. Though everywhere seemed deserted we moved forward cautiously across the overgrown lawns, ready to turn and run in an instant. Nothing happened. The ruin shimmered in the heat. We reached the first stones and David scrambled up to a tumbledown terrace.

'Come on!' he hissed. 'Come and look at this.' Christine and I joined him, to stare in wonder at a pit stretching out beneath our feet with areas of cracked blue tiles clinging to the walls and floor.

'What is it?' I asked

'A swimming pool, I think.' David jumped down and soon all three of us were in among the rosebay willow herb and brambles, picking our way through the earth and rubble to stand in the deep end and throw loose tiles against the walls to hear them smash. I only threw broken ones; stroking the glossy surfaces of whole tiles and putting them down again. I knew about public swimming baths but this one, miles from anywhere, open to the elements, derelict and glinting in the sunlight, seemed a magic place. Eventually we returned to the stream, walking back boldly down the drive since we now knew the house was a ruin and completely deserted, and settled to harassing the minnows and sticklebacks.

The remains of the building held no interest for us. We had already found an uninhabited house to play in, at the bottom of Beardwood Brow. When we tired of scaling the barn door of the farm next to it, in order to leap into the soft, sweet scented hay, the others from the top and me from the cross-brace part way down, we scrambled into the house through a broken window. It smelt of dust and decay and our entry set spiders scuttling. The ceiling had gone and the stairs had missing treads which we climbed carefully to reach the first floor and our favourite game:

balancing across the exposed rafters. I always went slowly, arms outstretched and feeling my way with my feet, not watching the flakes of plaster falling away below me until, with a rush of relief, I was across, and safe.

Looking back, I find it hard to decide what was the most dangerous thing I ever did, walking along those rafters or climbing on the roof. The worst injury I sustained as a child was a broken ankle, and that was from slipping off a two-inch high grass verge in the churchyard.

Our more urban excursions tended to be less exciting. Often we just walked across the bottom of the golf links to Christine's house in West Leigh Road, searching for lost balls and throwing them back onto the course as we passed, or sometimes taking one home to break open and unravel. If we went that way we returned over the tank, always visiting the top of the actual water tank to swing on the pointer and see if we could see Blackpool Tower before performing acrobatics on the railings intended to protect us from the long drop. I also liked to make my footsteps reverberate on the metal surface and clang on the steps up to it. From there we had a choice of routes home, but more often it was into the top of the park, either to clamber round the remains of the cannons, doing our bit to deepen the decades-old footholds worn in the soft sandstone abutments, or to climb the back wall of the old quarry around which the park was developed.

Once, as David and I wandered back home through the streets on the park side of Revidge Road, we noticed a dustbin overflowing with old books and stopped to look at them. The temptation was too much for us; he went home with a compendium of card games and I with a copy of *101 Things for Girls to Do*. My mother, who was horrified – her children scavenging in dustbins! – told us to throw them away at once, but when my father came home, he overruled her. The titles were respectable, the books worn but clean and still the kind of extras for which we had no money to spare. Mine became one of the favourite books of my childhood. I loved to be outdoors but I also enjoyed drawing, painting and making things, so this book was a treasure chest. It had everything from how to make a sewing chest from matchboxes to sticking paper shapes on young copper beech leaves to create green patterns as they grew. Unfortunately I never got that to work any more than I succeeded, a year or so later, in producing edible dampers over a campfire in the garden by following the instructions in *Scouting for Boys*.

Branch Lines

I always seemed to find, or be provided with, something to do, so boredom rarely figures in my recollections. The only significant exception is when, at the age of seven, I found the excitement of moving upstairs into the Junior School diminished by the reading lessons I suffered there. By that time reading was as natural to me as eating and drinking. Mother had taught me, alongside David, in the wartime evenings when she had also taught us both to knit, to use strands of wool from unravelled garments to make cords with tacks and old bobbins, and pom-poms with cardboard milk bottle tops – fun but futile activities indulged in by most of my friends – and a host of other things. I remember the stiffness of the green hands on the cardboard clock with which I learnt to tell the time; the grain markings and satiny feel of the thin, wooden blocks which fitted together to make coloured patterns and which Mother also used to teach me to count, and my favourite toy, not really a toy at all but a set of paint samples. These were cards which could be slotted behind a transparent panel in a piece of cardboard to show the effects of different colours in the various parts of a room, and their endless combinations kept me amused for hours. We never seemed short of indoor entertainment, which of course included *Children's Hour* on the wireless every afternoon and, always, books.

At first I had David's books: those he had been given before the war. *Orlando the Marmalade Cat* was a favourite, though my only clear memory now is of the black and orange picture on the front. I know we had a copy of *The Tar Baby* too, since it was the inspiration behind our efforts to melt patches of tar in the path across the top of the garden with a piece of glass. It also sorted out another of my early confusions over words in that it made me realise, eventually, that the black 'gastah' we talked about was actually gas tar. I had Puffin books as well, all of them far more advanced than the reader I was given by Miss Shuttleworth on my first day in Standard One, and I can still feel the unwonted boredom that induced.

I'm sitting on her right, next to the back seat on the row by the corridor but unable to see into it as I'm below the level of the glass panel. We've been told not to open the books that someone called Doreen is just handing out, watched in silence by 40 pairs of eyes. Most of us don't know her. She wasn't in our infants. I study her; small, though not as small as me, dark like me and with a serious face. Bolder than me since she's put her hand up and volunteered to give out the books even though she's new. I glance over my shoulder and catch Caroline's eye. We exchange a quick smile and I feel relief that she's my friend again and not

Betty's. For a moment the anguish and sense of desolation I suffered when they ran off together, pointedly ignoring me as they laughed and talked, and then hid from me, resurfaces. Shocked and hurt, I'd not known where to go or what to do but simply turned my back on the playground, leant against the wall – the wall now just below me – and sobbed into the cold brick. Caroline soon came back to me, but I feel uneasy sometimes, less secure.

Miss Shuttleworth's voice demands my attention: 'Open the books now and turn to the first chapter.' Eagerly I move the shabby red book out of the patch of sunlight sneaking through the tall windows on the other side of the room, open it up, flatten it out at the right page and begin to read. But not for long. 'John, start reading the first sentence,' is the next command. John reads it out and now she's asking Clive to read the next one, and Barry the next. She's clearly going to make us all read in turn, starting with the boys on the far side of the room. Now it's Kenneth's turn. I wait for trouble.

As he stumbles his way through the words I run my finger round the rim of the white pot inkwell set into the desk, then have to wipe it on the rough wood as both the finger and the inkwell turn blue-black. I watch dust drift in the shaft of sunlight, stare for a time at the bare front wall and the empty blackboard and pass on to study the picture hanging above Kenneth's head. I'm not impressed by it; just somebody standing on a shore looking at some blue boats. Briefly it makes me think of Cornwall, but my gaze soon wanders on.

Through the top of the narrow windows I can see the roofs of the houses in Clematis Street, which I pronounce Clemahta Street, as we all do. I don't yet know what confusion this will cause when I turn my hand to gardening. Now I just watch smoke blowing briskly from the line of chimney pots as Kenneth finally comes to a full stop. The next boy reads, and the next, but I'm no longer listening. I've counted the sentences and know which will be mine. In the shuffling quiet the sound of Mrs Eastham teaching next door penetrates the partition, though not clearly since the backs of the classrooms are together, we being the only ones who have to put the seats of our double desks up and turn round to face the speaker when all four partitions are folded back to create a hall for morning worship. I, however, no longer notice. I'm reading the book, though warily. Diana is reading aloud now, three desks ahead of me. I check I have the right sentence and await my turn.

Even though we were not allowed to take books home I had read the whole thing before the end of the second lesson, so all I learnt was how to do nothing in silence for long periods, and how to draw the picture on the wall from memory. Fortunately those reading lessons were not typical of the school and, if my first report is anything to go by, a handwritten testimony on a page torn from an exercise book which shows every subject as excellent, I was in no way disaffected as a result. Indeed few lessons have remained in my memory as that one has, perhaps because I enjoyed most of them, and school life in general.

It was as well that I was not easily bored. Though Christine remained a regular visitor and Caroline was soon old enough to walk to our house after school and during the holidays, as David grew older he developed friends and interests outside our home which no longer included me. Meanwhile, if my mother went shopping I went too, if she was baking I made mangled grey pastry, and if she was cleaning the house I stoned the back steps and window sill or polished the sideboard, but even so I was often left to play on my own. It was then that I developed my own secret hiding place that even David never found.

Roaming through the shrubbery in Whinfield Place one day, as I often did, enjoying the quiet green world with its leafy carpet, half looking for birds and their nests, I struggled through the growth round the bole of an old elm which was so thick and scratchy that we had never bothered to climb the tree. This time I persevered and discovered a hidden fork which offered a broad, comfortable seat and a fine view of everyone's comings and goings. David had begun to occupy our bedroom for a lot of our free time, first of all making models with Meccano and airfix kits, which I also enjoyed, but later constructing balsa wood aeroplanes which he sometimes fitted with pins and threw at me before hanging them from the ceiling. Now I had found a private space in which I could, in decent weather at least, watch, dream, wallow in misery or, best of all, read without interruption. When David was sent out to call me I could see quite clearly where he was, so stayed in the tree until he was safely back inside before climbing down and making a detour to conceal where I had approached from.

I read a great many books in that tree. As soon as I was old enough, seven I think it was, my father took me to join the library, which became my Aladdin's Cave. The three of us, that is my father, my brother and I, went to the library virtually every Saturday morning for years, borrowing the maximum number of books and returning them the following week, or perhaps keeping them for the permitted fortnight if they were non-fiction.

Access to the children's library was via a flight of steps in Library Street, through a revolving door and across a cool, tiled hall to reach the rectangular room which housed it. Double doors at the near end flanked the issue desk while bookshelves clothed the other three sides, with one or two tables and chairs down the middle. At first, unless I had a suggested title or author to search for, my selection method was simple; I started on the left-hand side, picked out from the array of linen-board spines anything that caught my eye or that I had heard of, and read the first few pages. If I liked it I took it, read all the books the library had by the same author and then moved on to the next shelf. Thus I encountered the obvious: Louisa M. Alcott, Enid Blyton, Arthur Ransom, Malcolm Saville and the rest, but also some of the less obvious in Norman Ellison's *Wandering with Nomad,* Evens's *Out with Romany* series and the Bunkle stories of E.M. Pardoe. As for non-fiction, once I had located the art and craft section, I rarely looked elsewhere. There was a particular book on drawing which I had on almost permanent loan until I graduated to the adult library, something I was actually given permission to do early when I argued – or rather my father argued on my behalf – that I had read everything I wanted to read in the children's section.

In addition to art, I took home books on knitting, making toys, raffia work and paper folding: anything for which I might be able to obtain the necessary materials. Seed & Gabbut's bookshop at the bottom of Preston New Road did well out of my spending money and choice of Christmas and birthday presents. I loved just going inside to drool over papers, paints and brushes and, of course, the books, though they were items I never thought of buying. Raffia I could only buy when I was older, at an art shop in Withy Grove in Manchester where my mother went for materials for the craft classes she later attended. Feltwork was one of the skills she acquired, as was leather work, which led to a fine, tooled, ration book cover and a pencil case which became mine when I needed one for secondary school. One year she made replacements for almost every lampshade in the house.

Although already competent, Mother had started going to sewing classes at the YWCA with Aunty Jessie during the war and, though her sister gave up, she later went on to more varied and advanced courses at Moss Street School and eventually the School of Domestic Science in Ainsworth Street. Like the rest of the family, she borrowed books to support her interests, but not fiction as we did.

The reference library and the reading room also opened off the Library Street entrance hall, the latter to the left of the broad staircase leading to the museum and art gallery with the librarian's office on the right. Wandering in and out to see if my father had finished reading the paper, I felt I had to tiptoe. Inside it, the only sounds were the occasional rustle of a newspaper from someone standing at the high sloping desks, or a snort or snuffle from one of the old men sleeping by the tables. David and I called them tramps, but they were just old, unkempt and frequently smelly people with nowhere else to go, not real vagrants who spent their summers wandering the countryside. The reappearance of one of those, whom we knew as Itchy Coo, marked the changing seasons. He spent his winters with the nuns at Nazareth House so regularly walked past Whinfield, ignoring our little gang as we trailed after him, shouting his nickname. In reality, with his battered hat, staring eyes, tangled grey beard and ragged black coat he frightened us, particularly if we met him on Meins Road or one of the footpaths, as sometimes happened, so in ones or twos we were not so brave.

We were much more tolerant of a different wanderer in the neighbourhood: Arthur, a harmless so-called daft lad, a bit older than us, who lived near Betty in West View Place. We either left him alone or gave him a friendly greeting. For a year or two he spent much of each day standing in the middle of the crossroads at Billinge End directing the traffic and I felt sad when he disappeared amid rumours that he had been locked away in an institution. In a similar way I also felt sorry for one of my classmates, Freddy, who was sent to the Royal School for the Deaf at the top of Halfpenny Brow on the outskirts of Preston when he was about eight. I believed he wanted to stay at St Silas' and used to think of him when we passed the place on the bus. Despite my addiction to boarding school stories, I found the idea of not being able to live at home and go where you pleased quite horrible.

There were some itinerants who actually came to our doorstep, including the knife grinder. When he turned up once a year my mother gave him knives or scissors to sharpen. I was allowed to watch him work and talk to him, but her reaction to the gypsies who travelled with the Easter fair and came trying to sell her clothes pegs was entirely different. I was shooed inside as she despatched them empty handed, stood on the step until they were out of sight and then locked the normally open back door. It was not left open again until the fair had been dismantled and the last caravan disappeared from the spare ground beside the River Blakewater at Salford.

Although the reading room where the undesirables dozed was adjacent to the children's section of the library, the adult section was not accessible from it, nor indeed from Library Street at all, but only via the entrance in Richmond Terrace. There was a connecting door at the back of the children's library, but that was for staff use only. Consequently my father left me and David at one end before going to the other entrance to select his own books. It was on these visits, as we waited for him to return, or to finish reading the paper afterwards, that I discovered the delights of the art gallery benches and banisters.

My father spent a lot of time with me and David when he first came home, but as his demob faded into the distance he ceased to be quite so much fun to be with. After 18 months or so I began to be wary of upsetting him and, for some time after that, despite our diverging interests, David and I drew closer again and became each other's confidantes and comforters in the aftermath of my father's increasing flashes of rage at our misdemeanours. We had no understanding of the increasing stress he was under: back from war to family life in a cramped cottage, short of money and unable to find satisfactory work. He left the debt collecting job he had returned to in Preston, worked in Greenwoods outfitters, became the manager of a fabric shop on Eanam which closed down and, worse, put money into some undisclosed venture only to be cheated out of it by his partner.

Nothing was said to us or in front of us. All David and I knew was that the kind, caring though strict father, who had always played with us and taken an interest in our doings, had become unpredictable and frightening. Not only did he lose his temper with us, he also began to rage at my mother and once, but only once to my knowledge, threw something at her: a cup which shattered harmlessly on the wall behind her but left me trembling in a corner in the shocked silence which ensued.

For a time, with my mother caught by divided loyalties, David and I not only turned back to each other for support, but even involved our friends. 'Betty,' I said one day to my classmate on the way to school, 'does your daddy shout all the time?'

'No.'

'Mine does. He gets really angry and shouts and I'm frightened and I don't want to go home.' As I spoke I felt the sense of betrayal which has imprinted this moment on my memory. I know exactly where I said it, can sense the spring morning, see the stones bulging from a garden wall beside me and feel the steep camber of the road edging the gutter beneath my feet. Words stir my memory in the same way as sounds and smells: velour, for example, instantly recalls the hullabaloo and guilt when I was so upset by David's jeering at a new hat I had just been treated to that I refused to wear it again; vicarious sees me clattering down the bus stairs clutching satchel, violin and book, being awed by a prefect using the word in deigning to speak to me, and looking it up when I got home. Similarly, the name Betty is sometimes all it takes for me to be a miserable little girl again, walking up Revidge Road in 1948. It was a particularly bad day – but I still recoil from raised voices.

Our personal peace was restored through the government's emergency training scheme for teachers. In 1949 my father enrolled at the newly opened college in Bamber Bridge, purchased a second-hand bike and, after 12 months of cycling there every working day and spending his evenings studying, qualified as a teacher. He was still under pressure, and went on to put himself under more pressure as he strove to improve his qualifications and prospects, but he soon had a steady job which he enjoyed and a steady income to go with it. His fiery temper remained, something my mother blamed on his Irishness – together with his untidiness and anything else he happened to do that annoyed her – but he was far less easily provoked.

For me life gradually settled down again. Unfortunately, though, he had already begun to lose David, who was becoming a rebellious adolescent and suffering for it. My father occasionally smacked my bottom, more symbolically than painfully, but frequently belted David. Most often, as with our attempt at running away, it was for his behaviour, but increasingly it was for no more than speaking his mind. The Victorian outlook my father never lost made him see any answering back by his children, or their forceful expression of opinions which differed from his own, as unacceptable, and therefore to be punished. He found fault with so many of David's attitudes and activities that my brother eventually stopped trying to talk to him about anything significant, taking refuge in our bedroom, talking to me or not at all. Sadly, as I discovered many years later, my father had known all was not well.

'I've brought up two fine children,' he said, 'but neither of them likes me much. What did I do wrong?' Taken unawares, I could find no adequate response, even though in my case he was wrong.

With our wartime isolation a thing of the past, not only were we going out and about, but we also had more visitors. People I did not know came to the house in the evenings, often to play cards. I was usually in bed and though I sometimes heard voices, as I had in Cornwall, I rarely saw the visitors. Uncle Frank, who went from the Air Force to the Police Force, was again a regular caller, as was Uncle George, not a real uncle but a friend of my father's who lived nearby in Duke's Brow. He used to walk down the lane, knock on the side window to announce his arrival and make a fuss of me once he was inside. Hence I remember him. David usually received most of the attention, so I also remember with affection a friend of my mother's, Mrs Ashton, who also seemed to prefer me. We went visiting ourselves, too, so I began to meet friends and relatives who were strangers to me.

We made occasional visits, which I did not enjoy, to a couple of elderly female relatives of my father's, or they seemed elderly to me. While the adults talked I was obliged to sit quietly in a corner of the stuffy front parlours of their identical terraced houses, near the chip shop in Limbrick, with nothing to do but watch people walk up and down the street on the other side of the lace curtains. I never knew who the ladies were or how they fitted into the family. The only interest they had for me was that they lived next door but one to each other but were not always on speaking terms, so we had to visit both to keep the peace!

Much better were the increased visits to my paternal grandfather. We had seen more of him as the war drew to an end and my father was home more often, but even though he lived in Clitheroe, having moved there from Blackburn in the 1930s, my mother had kept in touch with him during the war. A postcard to her father records her wishing that he could join us on holiday there. He took David to London to broadcast to my father on the BBC's forces request programme, so my brother knew him well. I did not, and nor was I old enough to register the deaths of first his wife and then his daughter, within two months of each other, in 1942, when my father was in South Africa. All I knew was that he had given David the toy soldier we played with, a guardsman about 3ft tall, rather obviously named Tommy, whose fur busby I used to sit and stroke before we acquired the dog. He was also the donor of my teddy bear.

Even after the war, travelling from Blackburn to Clitheroe was a significant journey for us, taking about an hour and a half to cover the 10 miles. The Preston New Road tram being a thing of the past, we caught one bus from Billinge End to the Boulevard to wait there for another one to Clitheroe. It was a long time before I learnt to associate the word boulevard with romantic, tree-lined, Parisian avenues. To me it meant a roughly triangular bus station in the middle of Blackburn enclosed by the Palace Theatre and the cathedral on one side, the railway station and its goods yards on a second, and the Adelphi Hotel and the back of Dutton's brewery on the third. With my image went the din of crowds, road vehicles and shunting engines, overhung by an industrial brew of petrol fumes, gritty smoke and the aroma of hops. That I did not mind; what I hated was the stench of rotting meat from the bone factory, which engulfed the whole town centre when the wind blew from the south-west or damp smog stilled the air.

I preferred Ribble buses to the Corporation ones. For a start they were red, my favourite colour, rather than inconspicuous green and cream, and they also had padded bench seats on the top deck with a channel beside them to race along, rather than pairs of hard seats on each side of an aisle. My ideal was the five of us, two and two halves and a dog, as my father requested when the conductor arrived with his machine to wind out our tickets, ranged along the front seat ready for another excursion.

Since Grandad lived in Whip Avenue we got off the bus at Primrose Bridge to walk through the paper mill and over the cobbled railway bridge to get there. The best bit was crossing the mill bridge, where we normally paused to count the eels in the river. On arrival I was always bothered by Grandad's greeting. He went through all the family names until he reached the right one, so I was met with 'Hello Eileen, Mary, Doris, Gladys, Joan.' It was worse for David. There were far more males in the family and no duplicate names, whereas a single Mary served for three females.

He was always welcoming and took an interest in me and David, but it was my parents he really wanted to see, especially his eldest son, home from the war. We were often left to our own devices and the toys and books we had taken with us. Roaming the house one day we found an accordion at the back of a wardrobe and carried it downstairs to have our curiosity satisfied. Grandad showed us how it worked and ever afterwards we rushed for the bedroom and the squeezebox as soon we arrived. We could produce no more than reverberating chords, but that was enormously satisfying. The adults talked for hours, sometimes forgetting we were there and turning to things not intended for our ears. When Grandad's possible remarriage first came under discussion I caught meaningful looks cast in our direction and the subject was changed, but not before I had heard that he was considering marrying someone called Gladys, a widow with two children of about our age, and that my father approved. I was not sure that I wanted my grandad to have other children.

Another of our Clitheroe entertainments was the children's playground on the green across from the house. It had two sets of swings, one with square roped seats for toddlers and one ordinary one, a see-saw, a slide, and two roundabouts which would give any modern health and safety inspector nightmares. One of these was a cone-shaped metal frame, which pivoted and swung from a central pole. It was about 14ft across at the base, with wooden slats round the bottom edge forming a seat 2 or 3ft from the ground. The other was a circle of a similar diameter 3 or 4ft above the ground with radial bars for handholds, straight sides and a footplate. The object with both of them was to push the device round as fast as possible and then jump on. Missing, and so being hit by the roundabout or falling on the gravelly ground, was painful. At first, to our chagrin, everything was chained up on Sundays for religious reasons, but not for long. Despite being a strong member of the Catholic Church, Grandad, who was also on the council, soon put a stop to that for the benefit of us and his new family.

I particularly enjoyed those early visits to Clitheroe when we went out in the afternoons. We visited people that Grandad and my father knew, walked around the town, the castle and its grounds or, best of all, on warm days, walked down to the River Ribble at Edisford Bridge with a picnic and our swimming costumes. It was where the locals went to swim but was never too busy, even when our group expanded to include Uncle Frank, Gladys and my new young step-uncle and step-aunt, John and Mary Dixon. Oddly, in view of our months in Cornwall, our father's proficiency and our mother's former success in competitive swimming, I could not swim at all and David got by with dog-paddle. That, however, was no hindrance to enjoying hours of splashing about, creeping into the edge of the deep pool or building piers or dams at the water's edge. I moaned about the walk sometimes, but forgot it as soon as I arrived. We always stayed late and, on the way home, as the bus throbbed through the darkness, I nestled sleepily against my father's protective arm, enveloped in the faint odour of cloth and tobacco which, for most of my childhood, breathed Daddy and safety.

It was in those early days at the end of the war that we also began to visit my mother's cousin, in Ashton-under-Lyne where my mother was born. She was another elderly lady living on her own with a very similar front parlour to my father's relations, rather dark and cheerless, though her house possessed a hallway rather than opening straight onto the street, but there the resemblance ended. The visit had two attractions, in fact three if you take into account David's growing passion for buses. This trip meant a train from the Boulevard to Manchester Victoria followed by a trolley-bus ride to Ashton, which he especially liked, and finally a local bus to her door in Welbeck Street. For my part I treasured the collection of gramophone records we were allowed to play as the adults talked.

Our own gramophone, inherited from Mother, was a square wooden box with an open turntable, a large, shiny trumpet on top and a winding handle at the side. David was more inclined to play it for the horrendous noises it made as it wound down, but I liked the music and was prepared to wind it up properly and keep it going. We had perhaps a dozen 78s, mostly of dance bands, which we played ad infinitum, although my favourite was a scratchy version of Ketélby's *In a Monastery Garden*. We also acquired one or two records of our own including *I Tought I Taw a Puddy Tat,* together with the sheet music for it, which David tried to play on his mouth organ. Cousin Annie, however, had an electric gramophone and far more records, including many of Gracie Fields. The one I played most was *The Biggest Aspidistra in the World.* She said I was to have them all when she died, but they never came my way.

What David and I really appreciated, however, was not in the house at all but in a nearby park: a lake with boats for hire. At first we all went, but once we knew our way around, David was given enough money to pay for boats and ice creams and we were despatched to chug, row or canoe the afternoon away as we pleased while the adults talked. We moaned about many of the places our parents trailed us round to – David more than I – but our rare visits to Cousin Annie were not among them.

Such outings were confined to Saturdays or holidays, as my father never missed a Sunday outing with Blackburn Ramblers if he could avoid it. It was my mother, therefore, who stayed at home sometimes so that David and I could pursue our own activities, mine mostly church-centred, his definitely not. We were never left in the house, either on our own or in the care of anyone else, as long as I was at junior school. This meant that as well as taking us out with the Rambling Club at weekends, our parents also took us to the social meetings every Wednesday evening, in the Reform Club on Victoria Street at the bottom of the market.

According to the 1937–38 syllabus these meetings began as discussion evenings. My father, for example, led something entitled *A Man's Money Value* and another was *Oh, You Women!* However, what I remember from the late 1940s are beetle and whist drives, ballroom dancing and home grown pantomimes and variety shows in which I eventually took part. Once, I recall, I wore a top hat and carried a cane to perform in a Fred Astaire and Ginger Rodgers tap-dance number, *We're a Couple of Swells.* All the acts were very simple. I remember someone called Jim who sang – usually *The Road to Mandalay* – and on one occasion another member, Fred Oldham, just shuffled onto the stage wrapped in a sheet asking 'Have you seen a funeral? I fell off!' which reduced the audience to hysterics.

I was not much interested in the formal proceedings – they were above my head – so I took a book to read and, once I was in secondary school, my homework, except at Easter. Even now, when I hear a cry of 'It's not fair,' I have to stifle the once standard Blackburn response of 'It's not t'fair till Easter,' for that was when the travelling fair arrived to turn the market place into a maelstrom of noise and colour. It came for a week, Wednesday to Wednesday, so from the Reform Club balcony I could survey both the transformation as it went up and the heightening excitement of its final hours as the rides thundered round faster and faster, the music pounded and the crowds shrieked ever more wildly.

The fair covered virtually all three and a half acres or so of the outdoor market, including the section along King William Street in front of the Market Hall, which was occupied by what were to me a few dull stalls selling pots and knick-knacks, as well as the much more interesting children's rides. These changed from time to time, but usually included a carousel with horses sliding up and down posts as it went round, a small wheel and a little dipper, all of which I was content with for several years. Beside the Market Hall came the cake-walk which I liked to wobble my way along and, despite the mats scratching my bare legs, I learnt to enjoy the helter-skelter which was erected at the other end of the fish market. Unfortunately most of the major rides, particularly the whip and the waltzer, and even the big wheel, made me sick. Being taken on them once was quite enough, though peer pressure made me try them again when I was old enough to go with my friends, with the same unfortunate result.

At seven or eight the dodgems, where I was awed by the skill with which the attendants leapt so casually from car to car to collect the money, and the caterpillar, with its fairly predictable motion, satisfied my desire for thrills. Indeed the caterpillar was my favourite ride. Squeezed in beside David, I gripped the rail in anticipation as the monster gathered speed, crashing its way up and down and round and round, until the moment came when the great, green cover began to rise and enclose us. I was deliciously frightened as the light disappeared apart from chinks in the rumbling, shifting floor, though I sat silently in the welter of shouts and screams from other passengers, hugging my excitement until the cover lifted and the world returned to normal. Most of the time, though, I was content to wander among the side shows and, when I eventually had pocket money, to roll a limited number of pennies on my preferred stall, playing only until I had either increased my initial stake or lost it.

Sometimes I walked through the fair with my mother during the week, but at the weekend we went as a family, our rides paid for by my father. Then came the real excitement as we pushed our way through the heaving crowds in a vibrant microcosm, unlike anything encountered in my normal grey environment. Roundabouts whirled, coloured lights flashed and voices fought the thunder of moving rides underlain by roaring generators which repelled me with the reek of diesel. At one moment the crack of shots drew my attention to the rifle range, the next I found myself cheering on a winner at the coconut shy or watching someone triumphantly carry off a glass bowl of doomed goldfish, all the time distracted by the cries of the showmen:

'Roll up, roll up. Only threepence a go!'

'How about you, Sir?'

'Come along, now. Don't be shy.'

As we dawdled along the row of booths where fortune tellers vied for custom with the fat lady and the flea circus, I well knew that money would not allow a go on more than one stall, and that I would certainly never see the inside of one of the booths, but I loved the whole experience. It was a blissful combination of noise, colour and movement – but for me, only during the day. At night I could only watch from my eyrie on the balcony as the coloured lights created a wonderland in the growing darkness. How I longed to be old enough to enter it, as David was allowed to do.

For years the closest I got to the fair after dark was the very edge where the hot potato man (who was also the hot chestnut man around Christmas time) stationed his cart for the week. On the final Wednesday, as we made for the nearby bus stop at Millets corner, outside the store where we bought ex-army equipment for walking, my father usually succumbed to the tempting aroma and treated us to a portion of potatoes. Briefly, as I waited on the crowded pavement, I felt part of it all. The rides roared behind me, the blinkered pony's harness jingled as he moved and the brass fittings on the cart reflected the shifting lights. The oven glowed red and gold as it opened with a blast of heat and the promise of a delicious potato, flavoured with coarse salt from the hinged, wooden box I had to stand on tiptoe to reach. I tossed my searing hot potato piece from hand to hand as we moved on, but by the time the bus arrived it was no more than a mouth watering memory of crisp outside and soft, flaky flesh within.

But the Rambling Club, which brought me so much pleasure, was far from the only one of my parents' activities in which I was obliged to join. In the course of his political activities my father met the Easthams, florists who were also heavily involved with the film section of Blackburn Arts Club. That subsequently became a short-term interest for all of us, and a source of unaccustomed boredom for me since when both my parents went to the meetings, I had to go too.

I recall gatherings in a room at one end of a gallery across the back of Fleming Square during which I was left to read, play about on the balcony or the wooden staircase leading to it, draw in the dust or watch the world go by and wish I could go home. The Rambling Club membership had a wide social mix, including some from whom I learnt a number of words my mother would not allow me to use – but not swear words. Since foul language was rarely heard in public, particularly in the presence of women and children, I never knew any. What my mother objected to was dialect. It was fine, she told me, for those who naturally used it, but not for me. I regret that I can remember virtually none of it, but what I do remember is the kindness shown to me by all the ramblers. They were like a family of extra uncles and aunts who talked to me, played with me and took me into their lives, and all their gatherings were social occasions.

The Film Club was different. Their members met to make and discuss film and I remember no other children at the weekly meetings, not even David, who had grown old enough to be left at home. On cold or wet evenings I took refuge in a corner of the cramped and dimly lit room, oblivious to the conversations around me, though they must have been concerned with the production of the romantic film in which my father played the male lead.

My father was a good-looking man with an easy manner and, unlike my mother, comfortable in any company. An RAF Brylcreem Boy, so much so that my mother complained perpetually about stains on the pillows, he also sported a neatly trimmed moustache and was always as smartly turned out as finances would allow. He regularly pressed the creases into his trousers – practically the only time he ever touched the iron, or any other piece of domestic equipment – and never stepped outside without polished shoes, nor allowed the rest of us to do so. I still feel ashamed if my shoes are dirty. So smart was he that standing outside the Town Hall during the royal visit to Blackburn in 1938 he was mistaken for a guest and ushered inside. Rather than cause a disturbance, he took my embarrassed mother by the arm, walked her up the steps, through the building and out through the back entrance.

The film in which he starred, *Then Came Isobel*, was made at Haydock Fold Farm near Mellor in the summer of 1949. It was premièred in King George's Hall and went down in history as the unit's greatest achievement, but though I can recall seeing it, and feeling embarrassed rather than impressed, as was often the case with my father's public activities, the actual making of it meant more to me.

For a series of sunny weekends David, Christine and I, sometimes with other children, frequently the daughters of my future headmaster, Mr McClellan, who was a co-director of the film, could play around on a farm without having to sneak into it. Not that David did much playing; he was busy being important as shot-board boy, signalling the different takes. Christine had become involved because Uncle Billy's newly acquired 1938 Austin Standard Flying 10 was also starring, being deemed more appropriate for a romantic departure than the florists' dark green delivery van, the only other vehicle available. At the end of the film the happy couple drove off alone into a black and white sunset, or at least they seemed to. Actually, since my father had yet to learn to drive, my uncle had to sneak into his place between takes and Christine and I were crouched on the floor in the back, giggling. No problem in a silent film. I was always particularly happy on days when the car was used since it meant that we had a lift at the end of the afternoon, instead of the seemingly endless walk up the hill to the bus stop in the village, or sometimes home.

While the actors were busy performing, the crew filming and the ladies providing and drinking tea, we children were generally left to amuse ourselves. Inevitably Christine and I played in the barn, as we always had at Beardwood, clambering over the bales, chasing each other and hiding in the scratchy, soft-scented hay. One wonderful day, however, instead of my cousin, I found a clutch of tiny kittens, squeaking and squirming in a hidden hollow. Delighted, I stroked the silky little bodies for a while with one finger, then ran to find my father. 'Daddy! Daddy! I've found some kittens. Come and look.' Back in the barn, he followed me up the bales and examined the tiny creatures. 'That's my favourite,' I whispered, touching a soft, grey head in the huddle of tortoiseshell and ginger.

'They're very young. Look, most of them still have their eyes closed. We'd better tell the farmer.' The farmer did not share my excitement.

'Kittens, eh! They'll be wild uns then. We get strays in t'barn and we've got enough cats of our own. Thanks. I'll clear 'em out later.' Horror drove me to speak.

'D'you mean kill them?'

'Aye, and if I don't they'll likely starve to death. I don't reckon their mother'll be back now you kids have messed with 'em. Even if she is, I'll not be feeding 'em when they grow up.' Dismally I visualised the shifting bundle, remembered their soft helplessness, and felt my father's hand on my shoulder.

'Couldn't we just have one?' I pleaded, trying not to cry, 'The grey one, Daddy, please can I save the grey one?' My father looked at the farmer.

'Tha'll have to tek it today, then. They'll be gone in t'morning.'

'Come on then. We'll go and ask your mother.' That meant he was on my side, so my mother's instant objections – that she was the one who would finish up training the kitten and looking after it, that it was too young to be fed or would just be killed by the dog – were soon dealt with. That day, with the kitten safely snuggled inside my treasured lumber jacket, not for once a home-made garment but a gift from Uncle Frank from a wartime posting in Canada, the walk up the hill was no trouble. All I noticed was the pressure of the little paws, the warmth of the furry scrap climbing all over me, the beat of its tiny purr and, occasionally, the glimpse of a grey head trying to escape through my collar.

Mother did, of course, finish up taking care of Smoky, as we named the newcomer, but the kitten readily sucked milk from a finger and soon a saucer. As for the dog, initially allowed to investigate her from the other side of the fireguard, he eventually became her protector, though whenever she climbed into his basket, he jumped out. Thwarted, she retreated to her favourite spot on the flap of the unused top oven. There she slept, warm and comfortable, but safe from the sparks which frequently singed both the dog and the hearthrug he went to lie on, producing a distinctive and unforgettable odour. She went on to have several litters of kittens of her own, which my father duly drowned in a bucket on the front wall. I soon learnt to accept it, but years later, when I read Seamus Heaney's poem *The Early Purges*, it was my own initial distress that I saw in the text, not his. However, it was not the drowning but the keeping of one of the kittens to give to a friend which probably led to a recurrent nightmare from which I suffered.

Smoky brought in a live mouse for the kitten to play with and, though my mother was not too keen, my father said we should let her teach Ginger – we excelled at unoriginal names – to catch it. Thus he shut all the doors into the passage, blocked them with the home-made rag rugs that covered the bare boards between them and the matting carpet strip, and let the cats continue. David and I established ourselves on the stairs, craning through the banisters to watch the performance. Smoky repeatedly released and recaptured the mouse for the kitten to chase, until it was dead and the kitten left mewing piteously over the corpse. At this point my father reappeared and disposed of it. Mother stayed well away and we kept no more kittens.

At the time I watched everything eagerly, but for several years afterwards I sometimes awoke, screaming and sobbing, from a dream in which I was a midget, alone in the passage, being threatened through the banisters by gigantic, snarling cats.

Personal Tracks

I spent more time with my parents and their activities than my brother did and appreciated them more, perhaps because he was older when my father was demobbed and we began to have a social life as a family, but also because I was a girl and so allowed less freedom. Nevertheless, my independent social life began to develop at about seven when, among other things, I joined the Brownies. Caroline joined too – we were inseparable then – and many more of my school friends, but though it was St Silas' Brownies, the pack included a few girls from other schools.

In my second year I remember being asked to collect an unknown younger girl from a house on Revidge. Feeling quite important I made sure my uniform was in order: brown tunic neatly held in place with the official, buckled belt; orange triangular bandage carefully folded into a tie; cap straight on my head (the proper shape but knitted by my mother for cheapness) and off I went.

I found the right house, rang the bell rather nervously and collected the new girl from her mother without finding much to say. Talking to her on her own was easier and eventually we became friends, although I have forgotten her name which is perhaps no bad thing in view of what happened. However, that first evening she was almost as quiet as I was as we walked down New Bank Road to the school. Everything went well until the very end. As we gathered together and quietened down for the departing prayer, waiting for the familiar 'Hands together and eyes closed, Brownies,' there was a sudden awful silence, broken by a gentle trickling sound from across the circle. I watched in horror as a puddle appeared at the younger girl's feet. I felt so ashamed, so responsible. I realised she had been too scared to ask to leave the room or where the lavatory was. Should I have told her? I had brought her and still had to go back with her. What would I do? What would I say? I felt very sorry for her, but also for myself.

The rest of us were immediately despatched to our corners and the weeping newcomer whisked away with a quiet 'Come with me. I'll show you where it is,' in place of the telling off I thought she might get. Brown Owl behaved as if nothing exceptional had happened and so, when my mother appeared to take us both home, I almost felt that nothing had. I told her about it of course, and since I have retained an image of that sad little puddle slowly seeping into the floorboards of Miss Lupton's classroom, it clearly made an impression, but Mother had no need to point out the virtue of acceptance and lack of fuss.

Joining the Brownies also involved me more closely with St Silas' Church in the way of regular church parades, attendance at festivals and, for a brief period,

Sunday School and Children's Church. For the last two organisations my father's stipulation that if David or I joined anything we had to stick at it for a reasonable length of time and attend regularly was suspended. He was as happy for me to go when I felt like it as he was for David not to go at all, and never went near the church himself. Fortunately, since I only attended because my friends did, I soon lost interest and decided that I preferred going out with the Rambling Club, so releasing my mother to go too.

This freedom of choice did not apply to the monthly church parades, however. As a Brownie I was expected to join the rest of my pack, together with the Cubs, Guides and Scouts, to march from the school gates to the church for Morning Service. We sang *The Teddy Bears' Picnic* out loud all the way along St Silas' Road to keep ourselves in step, and then in our heads once we rounded the corner, a trick which served me well much later when I joined the Officers' Training Corps at university and found myself one of the few recruits who could march.

I did not go to church every month – my mother liked her rambling too much – but when I did I thoroughly enjoyed it; at first proudly carrying my Brownie staff and later, as a Guide, the heavy flag in its leather holster, although I never quite lost my nervousness in parading down the aisle and negotiating the steps to the chancel. Part of my pleasure lay in participating with my friends, something which was equally true of the much more elaborate annual Whit Walks. They were associated more directly with school and an occasion for pretty frocks and bonnets, no longer expected to be white. I was delighted with a pink and blue check one Mother made for me one year, and the bonnet to match. Though not inclined to boast, she did claim to have been the first person in town to design and make a particular style of Dutch bonnet which was briefly popular.

Our parades, however, were insignificant compared with the Ragged School's annual picnic. Every year, drawn by the sound of the band, David and I rushed to Preston New Road to watch as the entire school and its associates neared their final destination, a field just down the road. It was a magnificent display with rousing music, marching men struggling to hold down a billowing banner stretching right across the road and a massive, motley procession behind. I found it just as entertaining as the annual veteran car run to Blackpool, which we also watched from the roadside.

We ourselves had extra church parades for religious festivals such as Easter and Mothering Sunday, the one service that Mother regularly attended. Was she a believer? I really do not know. She showed little sign of it, though she owned a Bible and kept a framed copy of Dorothy Frances Gurney's well-known words about nearness to God in a garden on her dressing table. I also had a picture book of Bible stories when I was small; vibrant pictures which I remembered and thought had come to life as I travelled through the interior of Yugoslavia in 1969, in an area which is now Montenegro. As the sun went down I found myself in an identical world of swarthy, robed men shepherding scrawny animals home to primitive villages along dirt tracks. It looked idyllic, but having to escape from a hostile crowd demanding money and cigarettes only to be forced to pay a fine for alleged speeding at five miles an hour soon shattered the image. I became uncomfortably aware of the difference between the interior of the country and its coastal resorts such as Dubrovnic, and was not surprised when war broke out in the region.

But religious associations or no, being a Brownie was fun. Though I was nervous going to strangers' homes to take the tests, I revelled in doing and making things to earn my badges, joining in group activities and performing in the shows we gave. There were outings, too, including a picnic on Meins Road which Caroline nearly missed because of our antics. Straying from a nearby birthday party, we climbed a wall and jumped from a tree to get into Witton Park. I ripped the exquisitely smocked dress my mother had just completed making for me; Caroline sprained her ankle. I had to live with my guilt and a patched dress, she with her pain and the prospect of missing the picnic. She was so upset that someone rooted out a battered, wicker bath chair so we could push her there.

It was about this time that my mother, worried about my shyness and lack of confidence, sent me to dancing class, having come to some arrangement with her friend, Winifred Boderke, who was joint proprietor with her sister of the Hindley School of Dancing. Thus I was able to appear as a dancer in the Brownie concerts, not all of which were held at St Silas' School. Though it did possess a stage, in that all five upstairs rooms were divided by partitions which could be folded back to reveal Standard Five's classroom on a platform above the rest, it had limited facilities. Leamington Road Baptist Church, where the Junior School had been housed during the war, had a better stage which was the scene of my first public performance. A very scared child, I slipped from a wooden toadstool to dance a solo as a pixie, dressed in tights, a perky hat with a feather and a green-and-brown tunic.

As a cure for shyness dancing class was a failure, not even increasing my confidence much on stage, let alone off it. I was still overcome by nerves some 20 years later performing in the chorus of an amateur production of *Orpheus in the Underworld*, but dancing did play a great part in my early life. As little boys in those days wanted to be engine drivers, so little girls fancied themselves as ballerinas and, tomboy though I was, I was no exception. Indeed I carried on dancing until I was about 16, and some pieces of music still fill my head with visions of barre exercises in an airy, L-shaped, mirrored studio on the top floor of an otherwise gloomy building on the corner of Astley Gate. Or perhaps that is not quite true.

The middle floor of the building was occupied by the amiable, young proprietor of a marionette show, whose door was usually open to the dim landing. Our parents often paused there for a breather on their way up the steep stairs while we dancers were always welcome in his large, dusty room, which was anything but gloomy. For a start the workbench where he manufactured his dolls ran below wide windows, but in addition, it was a gallery for his marionettes. Ranged along the walls in all sorts of costumes, sometimes clattering into dance themselves as a breeze caught them from the hallway or an open window, they dangled from their strings in a colourful confusion which delighted me. He used to let us touch them and tell us their names and what parts they performed. I longed to see one of his shows, but never managed it.

Once David had left St Silas' I regularly walked to school from the top of the lane with the same Betty to whom I had confessed my fear of my father, sometimes collecting another classmate, Anne, on our way down Woodbine Road. If we were early her father occasionally gave us pennies for reading to him. When the time came I remembered his kindness and gave him my insurance business. For me those pennies meant sometimes being able to buy the unrationed kali (our name for lemon sherbet) and liquorice root that other children regularly bought from Margerisons, the sweet shop in the block of shops opposite the post office in New Bank Road. Sometimes my mother gave me a twist of cocoa and sugar to take to school as well as my lunch, so that I would have something to lick from my finger and not feel left out. Lunch, the mid-morning snack for playtime, was always something she had baked, but once school meals were available, I had dinner in school.

Caroline and I had another source of income for a brief period, until authority intervened. A local milkman, Tom I think he was called – though that might have been his horse – used to stop his cart across from the school at dinner time, drape the nosebag over the horse's head and then climb back into the cart (quite a small affair with a central back step and bench seats down each side) to eat his own dinner. We often went across to pat the horse and chat to him, and one day he let us collect the cans and jugs for him from the nearby doorsteps. On our rambles I had seen lots of farm dairies, lingered in their doorways, been given warm milk fresh from the cows and rested on the stone slab platforms from which the churns were collected, but domestic delivery was a new aspect which intrigued me.

Our milk came in bottles, rattling down the lane in the Co-op van to be exchanged for the coloured tokens Mother put out on the back step to indicate the number of pints or half pints he should leave. Now I watched intently as Tom carefully ladled the creamy liquid from the battered metal churns into a hotchpotch of enamel cans and pottery jugs, which Caroline and I then returned to the doorsteps. That required careful walking across the uneven paving and over the shallow, hollowed step at the start of each short path, holding the containers with both hands as some of them were very full. Fortunately for us the metal gates had been removed with the garden railings as part of the war effort.

It was splendid having something to do and feeling useful and responsible, so naturally we went back the next day. This time, once we had done the three or four closest deliveries, we scrambled up onto the cart, the milkman clicked his teeth and the horse, still with the reins lying across his back, plodded on a few yards to the next group of houses, stopping of its own accord so that more containers could be collected and filled. I was amazed that it knew where to stop.

The whole activity was great fun and soon the two of us were regularly joining Tom after dinner, travelling as far as we could without being late back, and being given a penny or two for doing it. This went on until he replaced the horse and cart with a big, blue open car with the churns stashed in the back, where we perched on the folded hood. Perhaps someone thought that was dangerous and gave us away, since the headmaster stopped us shortly afterwards, but I was not too sorry. The battered and stained car was far less attractive than the horse and cart, and it also stank of sour milk.

Our ordinary dinner time excursions regularly included supporting the exchange of abuse with Sacred Heart School, just along St Silas' Road, but one day things went a little further. There had been mutterings and whispers all morning:

'There's going to be a fight.'

'Everybody's going.'

'Where?'

'Who?'

'I'm going if you are.'

Caroline and I listened excitedly. Dinner eaten, we dashed out to the playground, but to our disappointment no one seemed to be going anywhere. Then, just as we had given up, we noticed some of the older girls setting out in twos and threes to join small groups of boys who had appeared by our gate, heading towards Granville Road. We looked at each other uncertainly for a moment. 'Come on,' Caroline urged, 'We can't miss this,' so we ran to join the stragglers, others joining in behind us so that we were soon being carried along in a shifting stream of excited children.

On we tramped, down past the butchers, the greengrocers, the sweet shop and the hairdresser's to turn left round the Co-op where I was often sent to buy our milk tokens. No need to remember my mother's dividend number that day, as we swept past and along Granville Road before turning right towards the delph. This was an area of rough ground and derelict air-raid shelters at the top of Adelaide Terrace where, a year or two later, I would be very startled to receive my first kiss, a quick peck from one of the boys now milling among the crowd around me.

Now, though, I realised it was to be our battlefield. Drawn on by the drum of feet I was gripped by a sense of purpose. In the charged atmosphere I no longer cared what would happen. Feeling exhilarated and powerful, secure among my classmates in the anonymity of the jostling crowd, I lost all trepidation and marched boldly into battle.

Actually, the battle never took place. As we reached the delph and sighted the approaching enemy, St Barnabas', the front ranks also sighted teachers from both schools standing in wait for us. They had no need to do or say anything. As word swept through the crowd our forces scattered into retreat, now anxious only to avoid identification.

I cannot remember anyone being punished for this episode. In any case, physical punishment was rare at St Silas'. I was caned by Mrs Eastham in Standard Two for talking in class, but all that entailed was two taps of a ruler on my outstretched palm. The punishment was shame more than pain. The school's punishment book records that the headmaster infrequently administered one or two strokes of the cane for severe offences, but not on this occasion, and we remained free to come and go in the dinner hour. Indeed, when we reached Standard Four, at the age of nine, Caroline and I became so attached to our teacher and future headmaster, Mr McClellan, that every day we walked up through the park to meet him as he returned from dinner at his home on Revidge. What pests we must have been.

All too soon, however, we were in Standard Five, and it was my turn to suffer Miss Middleton. When I reached her class I found that the first lesson was devoted to sorting out singers. She made us sing individually in class, a dreadful embarrassment in itself, and sorted us accordingly. Any she termed grunters, mostly boys, were lined up against the wall and forbidden to sing again, in singing lessons, morning assembly or church. I felt sorry for them. I enjoyed and knew by heart the hymns we had sung every morning on our progress through the school. Now I found a new pleasure in learning songs from *The National Songbook,* apart from *Farewell Manchester* that is, which even as an unsophisticated 10-year-old I thought an aberration. Since the top classroom doubled as a platform for assembly it held a piano, hence the possibility of singing lessons, and Miss Middleton was, after all, the choir mistress. However, as I soon discovered, the standards she demanded, and her system of punishments, meant that not everything was so enjoyable.

A clip round the ear or a slap on the legs was not unusual, and in general any girl who offended her was made to sit among the boys and vice versa, but for some offences she had special tricks. If a boy forgot to invert his fractions she inverted him, dangling him by his feet if he was small enough. The whole class was delighted when one of our number proved too big and heavy for her to handle at all, though we had to contain our glee until playtime. We girls were spared this humiliation as our dresses would have fallen over our ears and revealed all, but Miggy had an alternative treatment for us. I quailed whenever I was summoned to the front to answer for my mistakes.

'See!' she would begin, grabbing a lock of hair and pulling my head down onto her desk. 'Look,' tug, 'at,' tug, 'that,' tug. Until she let go I could, of course, see nothing but the wall.

Boys did seem to get the worst of it. I accepted her treatment as part of life, but even so I was shocked when she threw Kenneth's satchel out of our top floor window, scattering his belongings in the rain. I forget what he had done, probably something as disproportionate to his punishment as my brother's being sent home in the snow for his tie some four years earlier.

But life in Standard Five was not all misery, and at least Miggy seemed to bear no grudge against me for my brother's offences. Caroline and I were soon monitors and graduated from filling the inkwells to the sought-after position of staff tea makers. This was far from arduous, since the staff numbered six, including the headmaster. Being a tea monitor offered two major perks: being released early from the lesson before playtime every day and being sent off to the post office from time to time to replenish the supply of Rich Tea biscuits, which needed no coupons. Sadly, we were sacked before the end of the year. Once the tea was ready we usually lingered in the small room at the top of the stairs which was all the space the staff had, the headmaster's domain being no more than a desk in the corridor, but we sometimes sat on the wooden steps leading up to the classroom door. Remembering how I used to play marbles with pills in my grandad's shop, I soon realised that we could do the same thing with the staff saccharines. We were sitting on the steps one day, doing exactly that, when Miggy heard us and opened the door.

Missing teaching time at the top of the school seemed to be no more detrimental to my education than dreadful reading lessons had been at the bottom, perhaps because we normally worked so hard. The first lesson every morning was a comprehension exercise which was lying in wait for us when we arrived, passage on one board and questions on the other, but we still read round the class before we started. Now, however, we were required to wrap our tongues round verses from the Bible, so I was not tempted to read on to the end. In fact I had acquired a liking for reading aloud which I have never lost. By that time the whole class could read without much difficulty, so it was pleasantly painless. We could all memorise things easily, too, having practised on the Catechism which we were obliged to learn. This was otherwise a particularly pointless exercise for me. David had been christened but I had not – a wartime oversight I was told – so I was not eligible for confirmation. Nor, apart from the acquisition of moral values, or perhaps more properly the reinforcement of those presented at home, do I think I was a particularly apt pupil as far as religious education was concerned. When Miggy asked me in class where Heaven was I brought the full weight of her scorn and wrath down on me by answering, 'In the sky.' I also failed to understand her sarcasm on a class visit to church for a sort of civilian naming of parts: aisle, pulpit, nave and so on.

'That's right', she said, as a metallic clang broke the profound silence. 'Kick the umbrella stands as you pass them.' I was one of the many who then did so.

Nevertheless I was, according to Mr McClellan's remarks to my father, in a particularly bright class. Apparently we had grasped everything we needed to know and worked through all the old exam questions well before it was time to take the scholarship exam – known elsewhere as the eleven plus – and he was struggling to find material for us. Even Miggy relaxed occasionally. I can remember one English lesson including a punctuation puzzle to amuse us:

> If the B mt put:
> If the B. putting:

The solution could be found by pronouncing all the punctuation, with a capital letter being replaced by the rather archaic prefix 'great', which gives 'If the grate be empty put coal on, if the grate be full stop putting coal on.'

Sadly for me, nothing stopped her giving us a spelling test every morning, so I had lots of very short playtimes as I struggled to copy out each correction 10 times on a scrap of paper about three and a half inches by four, before being allowed out. Fortunately this did not count towards the weekly position in class which determined where we sat, so I was usually at the back, safe from her swipes.

Apart from scripture lessons and the three Rs, we had physical education lessons in the form of joint PT exercises and team games in the yard; history and geography, which largely involved colouring in maps and putting place names on them; and nature study, for which we never left the classroom, though we did grow beans on blotting paper, and bulbs for the annual show in King George's Hall. We also had art and craft, which I liked (my prize product was a glove puppet made from a pencil, a ball of papier maché and an old piece of red corduroy) and sewing, which I did not like.

Mother had seen to it that I could sew. In making miniature sacks to fill the wagons of David's toy train I had even learnt to use the treadle to operate her beloved Jones sewing machine which occupied the space below the window in the front room. I was happy doing embroidery, too, but I had not inherited her general love of sewing and St Silas' lessons did little to promote it. I made three items, or perhaps I should say had to execute three tasks, since choice did not enter into it. The first was a cross stitch sampler which I was quite happy with, the other two a matching set of nightdress case and handkerchief sachet in a hideous shade of lime green. I do not know whether the material was provided by my mother from her store of remnants or by the school from the allocation of points it was allowed under rationing, but I do know that I would never have chosen it.

Miss Middleton was as exacting regarding sewing as she was over everything else. The hand sewn French seams had to be an even width and the chain stitched initials on the outside vertical and precisely placed using equal sized stitches, or they had to be done again until they were. The result was interminable stitching and unpicking, which was when I learnt that bloodstains from pricked fingers can be removed from needlework with a bit of chewed cotton. She was also insistent on the size of needle for particular stitches and even now, when my hand hovers over the choice of a needle for some task, her words ring in my head. 'That's not a needle; it's a poker!' Almost invariably I select the finer one.

Miggy also took the girls swimming – and how I wish she had not. The outings began with a crocodile along St Silas' road to the stop outside Cronshaw's Garage. There we lined up, still in pairs, to wait for the Corporation bus, which deposited us at Sudell Cross for yet another crocodile crawl to Blakey Moor Baths, during which my misery mounted with every step. There was not a single thing I liked about those trips. The entire building which housed the pool in its basement was grim, and the pool itself worse. The décor was drab green, the floors grey concrete; the chilly water stank of chlorine and the cubicles in the echoing changing room were cramped and uninviting. Even so, I stayed in mine as long as I could, that is until Miggy started banging on the doors. The reason? I could still barely swim and was terrified of both her and the water.

I always got into the pool as quickly as possible to avoid being pushed in, and did exactly as I was told in the hope that I would remain unnoticed. However, just as she had singled out the non-singers, so Miss Middleton now singled out the non-swimmers. I could just about manage a floundering breadth in the shallow end on a good day, grateful for the knowledge that I could touch the bottom if necessary, but that was not enough. 'Joan Ryan, you can do better than that. Do it again', came the strident command above the swirl of accomplished swimmers' mocking splashes as I struggled from one side to the other. So I did it again, and again, and several weeks later achieved the success I dreaded – Miggy believed I could swim a length. Next it would be into the deep end to follow the long, hooked pole she dangled a foot in front of her victims as she stomped along the side in her tweed suit, shouting threatening encouragement. I can see that moment now.

It's my turn. I'm standing at the front of a short line of shivering girls, cold from fear as much as temperature. My stomach flutters as I see the person in front of me touch the far end. Miggy turns to walk back, but though I know this is the signal for me to climb down the steps, I cannot move. 'Come along, Joan. In you go!' she thunders. Shakily I move across the damp concrete and start down the metal rungs. They bite into my feet and I shudder as the water rises coldly round me. There are no more steps. I turn on the last one to hang out over the green abyss, clinging tightly to the rail with one hand. She's got me this far, but now I can't let go. I'm too scared. I don't want to drown. 'Hurry up. You're keeping everyone waiting.' From the corner of my eye I see her moving closer. Is she going to push me? I take a deep breath, close my eyes and abandon myself to the churning water, arms and legs thrashing.

It's seconds later and I'm surprised to find myself afloat, but the far end of the pool seems an impossible distance away. I splash and gasp my way towards it, Miggy's pole tantalisingly just out of reach. I swallow water, cough and splutter. Her words wash over me, unheard. Desperately I wonder just how much water is below me and how soon I can put my feet down, gratefully grab the pole she finally moves within reach.

Before the end of the year I managed to swim a length, but with no sense of achievement whatsoever; just relief, and a lifelong antipathy towards swimming out of my depth firmly entrenched.

But I acknowledge my debt even to Miss Middleton's tyranny within the overall framework of a disciplined and caring school and staff. When the scholarship exam arrived, together with a ferment of excitement and fear, and the promise of presents from parents and friends for the successful, we were well prepared. Forty-seven of us took the first part of the exam, held in our own classroom; 33 made it through to the second part, for which we had to travel to Blakey Moor Boys' School, a much more daunting prospect. It occupied the same building as the detested swimming pool, as did the Technical High School David attended, so it was a morning off school and a trip into town.

I parted from my anxious mother at the gates and was relieved to spot Caroline's dark, curly hair and eager face as I followed the signs across the yard. As we went inside I rubbed the mascot in my pocket, a souvenir of Cornwall in the form of a tiny brass pisky, feeling increasingly nervous. We were sent to a classroom very similar to our own, smelling of chalkdust but with individual desks, not the double ones we were used to, and windows high above our heads so that we could see nothing outside. A strange teacher directed us to our places and we joined the other children sitting there in silence.

As the room slowly filled up I stared at the exam paper on my desk and the two neatly sharpened pencils beside it, getting more and more anxious, wishing we could start and get it over with. External noise died down as the clock approached the hour, and I began to wonder where my brother was. I knew he would be about somewhere in his smart brown-and-gold uniform, and I wondered if he was thinking about me.

At last the starting bell rang. Feeling jittery I picked up my pencil with a cold and shaky hand and studied the first question. Relief banished fear. There was nothing unexpected. I worked away, oblivious to the shuffles, the occasional coughs and the inexorable tick of the clock. When I finally glanced at it I was horrified. In sudden anxiety I lost concentration and tried to work faster. I knew I should finish the questions and check the answers, but time was short. I struggled on.

I was so keyed up about the exam that I almost forgot that the day was also my 11th birthday, but waiting for the results was even more nerve-racking. Of course I wanted the bigger bike I had been promised if I passed, but more than anything I desperately wanted to go to the High School. Christine was already there and I wanted to go too. My father had been disappointed that David had not gone to the Grammar School so I felt I had to pass. I was terrified of failure and what I perceived as the shame that would go with it.

Eventually results day arrived. As I waited to hear my fate I felt cold, shaky and sick. Caroline was looking anxious for once and Betty could only manage a thin smile as she saw me glance her way. There was not even much show of bravado among the boys. The wait seemed interminable, the tension unbearable as the headmaster finally entered. I gulped as he reached my name. For a moment there was a space where my stomach should have been. The world seemed to pause – then turn again. I had done it.

We were sent home immediately with the news and I did not even register what had happened to my friends. Once out of the door I broke into a run and did not stop running, or grinning, until I reached home. Over and over again as I had fretted my parents had said they knew I had done my best and the results did not matter. Maybe not, but what hugs and kisses I got when my success was declared.

Public Platforms

My father was an active member of the Liberal Party and on at least one occasion, the general election of 1950, spoke from the platform of the Community Theatre in Troy Street, the venue for a wide range of the town's entertainments and activities. I should have been proud, but still too young to be concerned about what was going on, I was more embarrassed than impressed, despite his enthusiastic reception by the audience. I need not have been. He enjoyed public speaking and was good at it, but on this occasion I sat with my mother in relative obscurity underneath the balcony at the back of the crowded auditorium, happy to be in an inconspicuous spot and wishing I had not been obliged to attend. Perhaps that is why I have never forgotten the local slogan: 'Don't be vague, vote for Hague.'

I was quite at ease with the theatre, but back of stage rather than front of house, as it was the venue for many of the dancing displays and competitions in which I took part. My dancing class held annual displays there and, although I inevitably had to fight stage fright, I really enjoyed them and was always among the first to volunteer for extra performances in other places. One, I remember, was in the girls' building of Wilpshire Orphanage, and another at Nazareth House, where I looked in vain for Itchy Coo in the audience of the homeless and infirm.

But not all my public dancing appearances were dependent on the Hindley School of Dancing. By 1949 I was already a member of the junior company of Blackburn Ballet Club, an organisation founded in 1937. Its premises were in Victoria Street, close to the Reform Club where the Rambling Club met, so I sometimes found myself going from one to the other. Although I enjoyed the dancing and the different company – the dancers came from several dancing schools – I was rather intimidated by the venue.

The narrow upper room, accessed via the Crown Hotel courtyard, lacked the brightness of Miss Boderke's studio, always seeming gloomy despite the inevitable stretch of mirrors on one of the longer walls which reflected the limited light from the grimy windows in the narrow ends, as well as our pirouettes. In addition it was often crowded with members of the senior company, men and women, or so they seemed, though they may have been mainly older girls and boys. I regarded them with almost as much awe as I accorded the president, Ninette de Valois, gazing down on us from her signed photograph on the wall. I was also wary of the teacher, Peggy Wilson, well known to many of the dancers as the proprietor of one of Blackburn's other schools of dancing, but a stranger to me. At first I even thought the dancing might be different, since I knew that her pupils took the British Ballet Organisation exams, which I was conditioned to think inferior, while we took those of the Royal Academy of Dancing.

However, the initially intimidating atmosphere of the Ballet Club failed to put me off; I was desperate to dance. From my first character appearance in a three-night run with the full company at the Community Theatre, as a troll in *Midsummer Night*, I gloried in the world of greasepaint and glamour. Although I fidgeted during costume fittings – not done by my mother for these performances but by the official seamstresses – hated the smell of theatrical make-up and the subsequent struggle to remove it, and wilted under the constant practice, once the show started it was all forgotten.

That first performance began with being called from the dressing room and conducted to the wings, tugging self-consciously at my costume as I went and checking with Diana, a St Silas' classmate as well as a fellow troll, that my hat was on properly. Once there I gave a last heave at my thick tights in an effort to get rid of the wrinkles, and was ready. As we waited, our whispers hushed by watchful adults, our attempts to peer round the curtains thwarted, I was gripped by nervous anticipation. With terrifying speed my slatted view of the stage showed me the principal dancers ending their duet, leaving at the other side, the corps de ballet reforming. It was almost time. The music changed. 'Now!' someone murmured.

Panic threatened, but before it could take hold I was moving, without conscious effort, into the brightness of the stage and an audience lost in darkness, felt but not seen. Fright left me. Greig's music flowed into my head and down to my feet as I executed the movements, played my tiny part in the performance and exulted in it. For the briefest of moments I was outside myself, not Joan Ryan performing a dance with four other girls, but a strange Norwegian troll.

There were four items on that December programme, only the second of them danced by the junior company, so I was soon on my way home through the ill-lit streets, holding my mother's hand, the music still playing in my weary head and completely captivated. In my dreams I was already a star of the Ballet Club and knew that I was destined to become a famous ballerina. There were more displays, more competitions and more full-scale performances in the next two years. The effort I put in was phenomenal – but stardom eluded me.

Soon, however, I had passed Grade IV in ballet and branched out into tap and ballroom dancing. My partner for the latter was a boy named Ian who travelled 15 miles from Nelson for his lessons as the proprietors of the dancing school were his aunts. They were also old friends of my mother's, whom she and I visited fairly often in the Victorian family house which the two of them shared in London Road. They were a rather old-fashioned couple but I liked them, found them easy to talk to and enjoyed my visits. I kept in touch with them long after my dancing days were done, retaining Christmas card and postcard contact with them until their deaths. It was through writing cards and thank-you letters to them from a very early age as The Misses Boderke, Miss Boderke or Miss Winifred Boderke, that I saw nothing strange in the terms of address in *Pride and Prejudice* in my first encounter with Jane Austen at the age of 12.

My mother also took me to visit a Miss Simpson, in a smaller but much smarter and more modern house towards the far end of Revidge, but that was not nearly as much fun. She had, I think, been my mother's superior at Rushton Son & Kenyon, so had to be treated with proper respect on what I now suspect were in part duty visits. I put her at the same higher social level as the people who lived in the new houses in Whinfield Place, and I certainly understood that I was on show. That meant best clothes, sitting still to avoid crumpling the antimacassar, speaking only when spoken to – which was not often – and the really hard part, not eating more than one of the tempting little cakes that came out with tea.

Ian's mother was another of my mother's friends and he and I also got on well. He was there for ballroom, not ballet – no Billy Elliot he – but was persuaded to try Scottish dancing and we became a double act with the Highland fling and the sword dance. It was splendid once we had learnt not to send the crossed swords skittering across the floorboards as we sprang over them. I found something extra special in dancing in unison with Ian, our heavy kilts swirling around us as we executed the precise steps and turns. Scottish tunes still set my toes twitching, bringing back the pleasure the dances gave me. Miss Boderke provided the hats, jackets and sporrans as well as the four swords, but Mother made our green tartan kilts. Even she struggled to pleat the yards of material required to make the genuine article, but at least I had good wear out of mine. It was my best skirt for several years, so did not go into my costume store in one of the big cardboard boxes which shared the space under my parents' bed with the chamber pot my father no longer used; a relic of his life with an outside lavatory.

Ian's mother, like Mrs Ashton, had two sons and enjoyed having a girl around to make a fuss of. As a result I saw quite a lot of the family, even staying with them occasionally, and became very fond of them all. I was upset when they went to live in Bournemouth, missing Ian's company particularly, though at 11 I still had no conception of the term 'boyfriend'. Though I had sometimes wished that two or three particular boys at St Silas' would join my regular playmates, I just had friends, many of whom were boys.

Completely undeterred by my lack of success in gaining any significant role in my dancing career I carried on, and in 1951 I eagerly accepted a part in the performance of *Merrie England* staged in the open air in Corporation Park during Blackburn's centenary celebrations. It was a magical event, eclipsing everything that had gone before, even though I was no more than an insignificant maypole dancer.

I thought I had practised hard for other events, but this bore no comparison. Learning the sequence of the steps was surprisingly difficult. Time after time we and our streamers collapsed from a rhythmic, swirling circle into a tangled heap of colour; someone had let go, moved the wrong way, broken the pattern. Peggy Wilson's voice rang across the room: 'Joan, stretch the streamer. Diana you should be facing the other way by now. Hilary, think what you're doing? You have to dance as one, not one after another.' But oh, the feeling when we got it right, experienced that oneness and watched the patterns round the pole change as we wove in and out in time to the music. But that was only the beginning.

This was a proper show, a full-blown light opera performed by adults, so eventually we had to attend rehearsals other than our own, to sit or stand about watching and listening as the cast learnt their lines, their songs and their moves. Sometimes I felt bored and tired as we waited our turn, but it was novel seeing adults being coached and reprimanded just like us. The show was produced by Ida Shaw, once Kathleen Ferrier's elocution teacher and a figure so well known in the town's artistic activities that even I had heard of her, and I viewed her with considerable respect. She was a stickler for detail and accuracy and, with the frequency of repetitions she demanded to achieve her aims, I soon began to understand what was going on and where we fitted in. I also began to know some of the dialogue and lots of sections from the songs as we sang along with the chorus – unheard of course – and then among ourselves when rehearsals were over.

We mingled with the adult cast too, sharing their breaks, being flattered by their attention and their approval of our dancing, being talked to and teased, treated as fellow performers. I soon recognised all the stars, but there seemed to be an infinite number of minor characters and chorus members, and there was even a live donkey. Regrettably its handler, though happy for us to pet it, was deaf to our pleadings for rides. It was all hustle and bustle, a heady mix of sights and sounds which brought the England of Elizabeth I to life on the park's grassy stage. That was specially built, more than twice the size of a normal one, its floodlights augmented by green bulbs suspended in the surrounding trees to bring out the colour of the leaves as a background to the imaginary village they pinpointed.

The performances were scheduled for three nights in August, with three more as reserve dates, and how anxiously everyone watched the weather. Two of the reserve dates had to be used, but on the opening night we were lucky. When the overture began the evening sky was clear and the audience stretched away up the hill in a comfortable temperature. It was a free show, and thousands turned out to watch. Since there were no wings to wait in, we performers clustered at the sides of the grass mound, outside the circle cast by the floodlights and so more or less out of sight of the audience but able to see them. I tried to locate my family but without success; there were just too many people, sitting or moving around to a rising background of adult voices laced with children's cries and calls. I was not even certain they were there. They had still been at home when I set out to run down through the park, and my father was not noted for being early for anything.

What I could not see, and since I was in it never did, was the full glory of the performance. I had glimpses through the crowd and could glance around when we were on stage but not dancing, but even then I had to concentrate on what I was doing. I knew as well as everyone else that an individual mistake could bring disaster, though the touch of terror that came with that thought only served to heighten the excitement. And it was exciting, really exciting, not in any single sense but in the whole experience. Never before had I performed in the open air, danced round a maypole, seen a musical show, shared a stage with an animal, worked with a crowd of adult actors or seen history brought to life in the presentation of an ancient village peopled by characters wearing strange Elizabethan clothes. There were men in smocks with floppy hats and staffs, others in tights and puffed out tunics, yet more with long beribboned coats and wigs, and all in brilliant colours, blues, golds and reds. There were women laced into wondrous crinoline dresses and given fantastic hairstyles, and we ourselves had pretty dresses, laced bodices, floating ribbons and bonnets.

On top of all this there was the music, supplied by the combined forces of Blackburn Music Society Orchestra and Choir. It was music of a kind quite new to me, not so much in the solo parts, nor even in the music itself, but in the power of the chorus and the depth and volume of their singing as it rolled out across the darkening park, magnified by microphones. 'Oh where are the yeomen, the yeomen of England?' the Beefeaters roared, and standing in the costumed crowd beside the patient, panniered donkey, I was lifted into another time and place.

At the same time, in distant London, the South Bank Exhibition was marking the Festival of Britain. Perhaps it being festival year had something to do with the choice of *Merrie England* for Blackburn's centenary show, but the national celebration had little meaning for me in a world without television. I saw brochures and knew that trips to London were available for those who could afford them, but its focus was too far away, too vaguely heard of and seen only in newspaper pictures or on the Pathé news in cinemas. What mattered to me was my town and its events, of which there were dozens throughout that summer, the main ones being listed in a souvenir brochure which also contained a comprehensive account of the town and something of its history, prefaced by a message from a very youthful looking Barbara Castle, MP.

As well as the performance in the park, the illuminations in it and the temporary fairground located there, the outdoor attractions included processions, sports fixtures of all kinds from football to bowls, a firework display and, taking place in Blackburn for the fifth time in its history, the Royal Lancashire Agricultural Show, which drew crowds to Witton Park for four days. That was when I first thrilled to the band of the Household Cavalry, gazed at animals being judged in the ring while wondering how anyone could distinguish between such magnificent beasts, admired the massive Brewery dray horses, brushed and beribboned for the occasion, and acquired a taste for watching trotting races. In the dog show Peter won the categories for shiniest coat and shortest tail (cheating really since his tail had been docked before he became ours) and the family cheered Christine on as she competed in some of the riding events. There was so much of it, such a variety of things I had never seen before that I wandered about in a daze. The event was so successful that Blackburn went on to have an annual show of its own.

Meanwhile, indoors, a cast of 50 presented Noel Coward's *Cavalcade* at the Community Theatre for six nights and Sir John Barbirolli conducted the Hallé Orchestra in King George's Hall, where he is reported to have reached down to remove a broken wire from the piano as he did so. Music, other than brass bands, was not one of my father's interests, so I was never taken to concerts, centenary or otherwise. Thus I failed to realise until long afterwards just how much my mother enjoyed music.

There were lots of minor activities that summer also, including exhibitions of art, books and textiles, and even a special centenary tropical fish exhibition. Everyone seemed to be involved in the festivities in some way. Every schoolchild was given a pamphlet containing a coloured picture of the town's coat of arms together with a detailed explanation of its features and a translation of the motto: Arte et Labore, by skill and labour. It also contained information about the establishment of Blackburn as a county borough in 1851, the earlier local event also coinciding with a London festival, the Great Exhibition in the Crystal Palace in Hyde Park. I kept the pamphlet for a long time, not particularly for the history, though I was intrigued by the heraldry, but largely for the picture, since I was more accustomed to seeing the coat of arms depicted in black and white, or even carved in stone on public buildings.

There were also special activities arranged for children, many of them quite minor but fun, of which I best remember a sort of treasure hunt in shop windows. Doubtless the shopkeepers envisaged increased trade from parents helping their children to search, but what I recall is chasing from shop to shop with my friends hunting for the number printed on our family copy of the souvenir programme. The prize was far less significant than the feeling of triumph when, close to the end of the competition, I finally located the number.

Adult shoppers could vote for the best dressed window and, during one week, the town had its own version of the men employed by newspapers to walk round seaside resorts in summer with a copy of the paper waiting for people to spot them and claim a prize. Our quarry, entitled Trader Tom and identifiable from a description in the *Northern Daily Telegraph*, handed out prizes in exchange for the correct phrase and production of a souvenir brochure. I was sure I saw him once, but I lacked the confidence to accost a strange adult.

The town's outdoor groups laid on a selection of some 15 cycle rides and walks, one or two of which I joined in with my family. Aunty Jessie and Uncle Billy were keen tandemists, just as devoted to the Blackburn branch of the Cyclists' Touring Club as my parents were to the Rambling Club, so we cheered on their friends as they puffed and panted their wobbly way up Shear Brow in the Hill Climb. I also made my second crossing of Morecambe Bay. This time coaches were provided so getting there and back was easier, but not so the walk. The channels in the bay had shifted so much that we had to cross the Kent into Grange by boat.

David went as willingly as I did for these special events, but in any case we had no choice over the one which my father organised and led, which we were caught up in from the start. That was the beating of the town boundaries. We were not actually going to beat them, that is carry sticks with which to thrash the boundary stones as was originally the custom, but simply walk the line which had denoted the limits of the County Borough of Blackburn at its inception in 1851. It was, in fact, very far from simple.

My father had to do five things: identify the boundary on the ground, check the route beforehand (which involved all of us at times and frequently other members of the Rambling Club as well), identify points where there were obstacles in the way, talk to landowners and liaise with the council over access and, finally, lead the walk on the appointed day. It took an enormous amount of time and effort but he was in his element, out day after day doing the walking he loved. Beating the Bounds, as the event was termed, became the focus of our household and of more and more interest to me as the day approached, even though it clashed with *Merrie England*.

I was already praying for good weather for my performances. Perhaps my father should have prayed too – although with his relationship with the Church success would have seemed unlikely – or at the very least crossed his fingers, for what we got was rain, not just light rain or showers, but a day-long downpour of such severity that, despite my enjoyment, my clearest memory is of being utterly and completely sodden. The rain was already drumming on the skylight when my father woke us in his usual fashion – by letting the dog in to jump all over us – and was still beating down when I fell exhausted into bed.

The day began normally with the usual porridge all round topped with golden syrup and milk, washed down with more milk in my case and tea by the rest of the family. Meanwhile we stared gloomily out of the window at the rain dripping off the coal shed and the stable roof opposite. Though we were all going out, and it was the middle of August, my father had lit the fire, but even with that flickering away and the light on it was still dismal. 'Come on,' he said eventually, swallowing down the last crumbs of the slice of bread and piece of bacon he always had in addition to his porridge, 'Let's be having you. You'd think we were going to a funeral. It's only rain. Go and get your boots on. We can't keep the Mayor waiting.' This was rich from him. He was always on the last minute and the later he was the slower and more deliberate his movements became. Meanwhile my mother became increasingly infuriated, dashing around to gather up the contents of his pockets which he scattered all over the house whenever he came in, punctuating her progress with varying cries of panic and protest:

'Vic, what are you doing now? Look at the time. Here's your pouch. What have you done with your pipe? I can't find it. The bus leaves in five minutes. You'd try the patience of a saint.' And all this after she had made sure that David and I were ready. More often than not my father simply ignored the tirade. Sometimes, when it was obvious he really was late and could not find something, he snapped back, but on this occasion, when she began to chivvy him, he contented himself with a mild,

'It's all right Mother. There's plenty of time. Just do what you have to do and leave me be.'

That turned her attention to me and David, both of us so looking forward to the event that we were actually ready, hence I was despatched to find the cat and put her out, David to call the dog and bring him in. He came with a distinct odour of damp dog, which spread through the house as he leapt about barking and waving his stub of a tail when he saw we were wearing boots. Mother sorted him out, then fussed about making sure we had all our rain gear, particularly the sou'westers, to go with our plastic capes, before packing some extra food in view of the bad weather. Meanwhile my father banked up the fire and collected his notes and maps. Before long we were on our way, well three of us were. Mother had failed. Having so many additional things to take my father had forgotten his walking stick, an accessory as essential to him as his pipe, so he ran back for it, almost missing the bus. He never went out rambling without a stick, but lost so many of them that my mother developed a habit of checking the area after every pause on a walk. I used to visualise the neglected sticks leaning against walls or trees for days on end, or lying on the ground as grass grew over them, and wonder if anyone found them and gave them homes.

I was already wet by the time we reached the bus stop, though only on the outside. My excitement had continued to rise despite the weather and David and I were both chortling as we chased up the bus stairs in a flurry of damp coats, boots and rucksacks, following Peter who was straining at his lead. Living at the terminus was good in that we almost always got the front seats into town, as we did on this day, heading not for the Boulevard and Queen Victoria's statue where we normally met for rambles, but for the Town Hall.

The walk was open to the public, the advertised meeting place at 9.30am at the starting point, the Yew Tree pub, about half a mile from our house. We, however, as the leader's family, were going to join one or two others for the official send-off, which largely involved a speech from the Mayor, the handing over of the map to my father – which he had in fact taken with him – and a photograph. Then, which was the highlight of that particular ceremony for me, we were loaded into an official car and driven to the start. I was delighted by it all, not least myself pictured in the evening paper on the Town Hall steps with the Mayor.

There were other fixed points and times along the 15-mile route, at Wilpshire, Knuzden Bridge, Bolton Road and Cherry Tree, so that people could join or leave as they wished. Thus, while there were always between 20 and 30 walkers in the party, they were not always the same ones. Even so, perhaps because of the terrible weather, they were for the most part Rambling Club members who were used to coping with the elements and laughed and joked the day away, and it did have some entertaining moments.

Even the start appealed to me as we had to climb the fence alongside Preston New Road into a field to the west of the Arterial Road before beginning to make our way north along the hedge. Sometimes we were on paths and tracks, but mostly it was mud, wet grass, barbed wire fences, prickly hedges and dripping woods. It was so awful it was ridiculous, so when someone slid to the ground and struggled upright unhurt but covered in mud, it was just something else to laugh at. Successful crawling under wire was applauded and nettles were thrashed out of the way with extra enthusiasm. It was only when we stopped that I noticed how wet and cold I was, and really became aware of water trickling down the inside of my collar and down my bare legs to soak into my socks. Otherwise I tramped contentedly along in my own warm dampness, the water squidging between my toes with each step. Frequently, too, relief arrived in the shape of the Borough Engineers Department refreshment van.

Details of the walk had included the need for participants to bring food, but promised that drinks would be provided. They were only supposed to be available at the four change-over points, but in fact the van appeared, like a wheeled lifeboat, almost every time we reached a road, dispensing not only tea but also sandwiches. Never since have I sunk my teeth into soggy sandwiches of sliced white bread and meat paste with such relish, never curled my fingers quite so lovingly round a steaming cardboard cup to gulp down rain-splashed tea. I loathed the taste of the cardboard, and even now if I cannot avoid a cardboard cup the first sip takes me back to that day, but it was that or nothing, and nothing was not an option.

In lots of places the 1851 boundary bore no relationship to the 1951 features and yet, as far as possible, we had to walk the line. Having been taught all my life that I had to keep to the path when crossing farmland, I took enormous pleasure in what seemed to me like licensed lawlessness as we forged straight across fields, climbed walls and walked through hitherto forbidden farmyards. There were just four children that day: me, David, Christine and my friend Alan, who was my age and whose parents were also keen Rambling Club members. It was a real adventure for all of us.

As well as the general obstacles we grappled with all day there were more specific ones – some expected, some not. First came a stream which, when my father reconnoitred it, had been no more than an insignificant trickle which could be jumped across. Even I quailed at the idea of paddling in water over the tops of my boots, so waited warily as he cast about for a way across what was now a small torrent. There was a bridge, a metal affair about head height, but access was denied by a dense, barbed-wire backed hedge. However, my father soon spotted that there was a ledge on the side. One by one we scrambled up and inched our way along the outside, clinging hard to the top rail which I could only just get my hands over. I loved it.

I also liked the novelty of walking straight over the railway lines which our route crossed, though they presented no problems. The next real obstacle in our path, the high brick wall of a mill yard, was seemingly impassable, but here I learnt that provision had been made for us where difficulties were anticipated. The mill owner had provided ladders, so it was up one side and down the other. Poor Peter was so wet and slippery, and whined and wriggled so much that my father almost dropped him as David climbed up and passed him over. I found it easy, even with slippery wet rails and a flapping cape, but there was lots of laughing and joking as some of the older and weightier members of party heaved themselves up and over the top. Mother was too busy telling me to be careful to worry about herself.

When we left by the unlocked yard gate I thought that was it, but joy of joys, outside was a boat, complete with boatman, waiting to row us across the mill lodge. The craft, which had quite ornate seats at each end and looked like one of the pleasure boats from Queen's Park lake, only carried four at a time, and as we waited, the steady rain turned to a torrent. I was surrounded by groans of dismay as the far end of the dam, where a few moments before, the straight, grimy-green bank had fronted the distant grey-washed moors, virtually vanished. When my turn came I settled myself on the wet seat, huddled into my cape and pulled down the front of my bright yellow sou'wester to deflect the force of the downpour from my face. It then dripped onto my feet, but I was still better off than Christine, who was wearing her school mac, which opened as she walked or sat, letting the rain soak through into everything she was wearing.

I thought that was probably the end of the fun, but not so. We had encountered the Leeds and Liverpool canal more than once and eventually we had to cross that too – miles away from any bridge. But the council had done their work well. No sooner did we appear than a flat bottomed punt affair, little more than a raft, was pulled across on a rope to ferry us to the opposite bank, six at a time. I was not so sure about this one and watched rather anxiously as one of the larger ladies, who had needed helping up the ladder, made it rock alarmingly. 'Sit down, Elsie,' someone called. 'Tha'll sink it.' I thought she might, and though everyone laughed and she made it to the other side without mishap, I still clambered aboard rather cautiously. Once afloat, however, sitting at the outside next to Alan, with Christine beyond him and David opposite, I spent the crossing quite happily trying to spot fish through the rain-spattered surface.

I thought that boat trip really had to be the last of the strange events, but there was one more surprise in store. Approaching Cherry Tree we reached the last obstacle, a house. It had been built right across the boundary, but the lady who occupied it had offered to let us walk through her passage and kitchen, and was standing outside to greet us under the protection of a large umbrella. However, because we were so wet and muddy, not everyone wanted to go inside. 'No, it's not right,' insisted the same lady who had unbalanced the boat. 'We're far too mucky and wet.' Heads nodded in agreement and there was some alarming discussion and hesitation. I had no such scruples. I was anxious to walk every possible step of the boundary, especially through someone's house. In the end, to my delight, most of us scraped the mud off our boots as best we could, shook the rain from our clothes and tramped through over protective newspaper.

The outing ended at Yew Tree as it had begun, the last sodden, bedraggled walkers completing the excursion about 7.30pm as planned. My father and the dog walked home from there, accompanied by others who were heading for the bus terminal at Meins Road, but not me. I had done what I wanted to do. Uncle Billy was waiting with his car to collect Christine, and as soon as he made the offer I was inside it too, very ready to be driven up the road with my mother and David for my steaming plate of home-made soup. Eventually, when the fire had been coaxed into enough life to heat the water, it was bath and bed, even though it was not bath day. Twenty-one people completed the whole circuit that day and so signed the official declaration – but there was no paw print for Peter.

Apart from marvelling at the concluding firework display, a spectacle unlike anything I had seen before, tapping my feet to the marching bands and gazing in wonder at the magnificently decorated floats in the final exuberant parade, that was effectively the end of my participation in the celebrations. But what fun it was. In a summer which saw warships in the Gulf because of trouble in the Anglo-Iranian oilfields, Guy Burgess and Donald MacClean disappearing behind the Iron Curtain and local Civil Defence recruitment drives based on the fear of attack, I was having the time of my life – and there was more to come.

Beyond the Barriers

The end of the centenary celebrations saw the beginning of the next clear period of expansion in my life, secondary school, which was not quite the daunting experience that it might have been. This was largely because of the physical separation of the first two years into a converted mansion, set in its own extensive grounds at the bottom of Crosshill Road. This meant that initially there were not many more pupils than there had been at St Silas'. I had further to walk: along the main road, over the low wall by Springfield Maternity Hospital (in which I had been born) down the well-worn path across the delph – not the same delph as the once intended battle site with St Barnabas' School, but a different patch of spare ground opposite the church – to Manor Road and the school gates. But it was still no more than a 10-minute walk, or the more usual five-minute run to avoid being late. Not only that, but of the entire intake, which must have been about 90 girls, 10 were from St Silas' and others I had met through dancing. From the very beginning I had no shortage of friends. It seemed strange at first without the boys, six of whom had passed for the Grammar School while another one, together with one girl, had followed my brother to the Technical High School, but I did not particularly miss them. Less than half the class had gone on to secondary modern schools, mainly Blakey Moor Girls or Boys.

Once the euphoria of passing the scholarship had expired, hard reality appeared in the form of information from the school about uniform and all the other bits and pieces which had to be provided. Now there would be no more of David's old jumpers unravelled and re-knitted for me, no more home-made skirts and blouses, no more well-worn coats I was growing out of. I was to go with my mother to Johnny Forbes and buy everything. Or so I thought. I was overjoyed. I had never had more than one item bought for me at once, and this was also going to be clothing that meant something.

St Silas' had once had some vestige of school uniform – the tie which David failed to put on in the winter of 1947 bore red and silver stripes and I had worn a school badge in the same colours on a red blazer at some time because the they matched it and my red sandals – but this was different. Not only was I going to have a complete set of new clothes, but they were also going to be the sign of my success. I was not quite as pleased and proud as Betty, who went on holiday in her new school uniform that year, even down to the bowler hat with its light blue and dark blue band, but it meant an awful lot. Unfortunately, it also cost an awful lot.

By this time my father was completing his probationary year as a teacher, so we had more money, but not a lot to spare. My parents having been through the problems of providing a uniform for David when money was even tighter, their first question after reading the list was what I might be able to do without, the second, what my mother might be able to make. She knitted the grey knee-length socks for which I made the elastic garters, and I was far from the only child who turned up in a hand-knitted navy blue cardigan rather than the smooth, purchased version I coveted for years, with a sky blue stripe round the front edges and cuffs. However, I was aware of no one else who had home-made blouses. I might have been embarrassed by them had my mother been less adept, but in fact I was rather pleased as she made one of them from viyella, which was delightfully soft and warm in winter. Only for special occasions, or if my collars were unbearably dirty, was I allowed more than one clean blouse a week. The pattern was bath night on Sundays, clean clothes and washing on Mondays.

So, one day in September 1951, complete with a smart satchel smelling of new leather and containing little more than a boxed fountain pen and propelling pencil set, coloured pencils in my mother's slightly unwillingly donated pencil case, a bottle of ink, and a piece of Chorley cake for my lunch, I duly presented myself at the gates of the long, curving drive which led to Crosshill. I had arranged to meet Caroline and Betty for moral support and, as we hung about watching the second years enter but lacking the courage to follow them, we were gradually joined by other friends seeking the security of the familiar, but in a way, we were already different.

Gone were the feckless girls who in July had joined the boisterous, diversely clad individuals thronging St Silas' gates until boys and girls were summoned to their own yards to line up and enter the building. Now, our solemn faces framed by freshly washed hair constrained by bowler hats, each of us wore a neatly belted gabardine mackintosh over a gymslip the regulation four fingers above the ground when kneeling and, below that, grey knee socks which disappeared into polished black lace-up shoes. Nor did the uniformity finish there. Satchels slung over one shoulder, we dangled navy blue shoe bags from the other hand, each made to the pattern we had been sent and complete with its owner's name embroidered on the outside in light blue chain stitch. (I had benefited from Miggy's sewing lessons after all.) Inside each bag was a pair of black pumps to be worn with knickers and vests for gym in the converted stable loft, netball in its yard and rounders on the misnamed field. Alongside the pumps nestled a pair of black ward shoes which we would soon find ourselves expected to change into and out of five or six times a day as we entered or left the main building. Inspecting each other, we lingered indecisively until, as so often, Caroline made the first move. 'Come on,' she urged. 'We have to go in sometime.'

I was less awed than some by the approaches. After all I had been living at the end of a similar drive since I was born, but in all that time I had never been further inside Whinfield House than the front porch. Thus, though I stared about me with interest as we made our way along the avenue of trees, it was the inside of Crosshill that was to be a revelation to me, and a place that I loved from the outset.

Since pupils were not allowed to use the front door we were led to the side entrance and down to the basement. There we located our pegs, left our bags and changed into our indoor shoes before being conducted to the hall. It was then that I first began to appreciate that I was in a different environment. A magnificent, honey-coloured staircase swept down from the first floor to the gleaming tiles of the entrance hall we crossed. Everything shone – not least the banister rail, which I was to discover owed some of its gloss to girls' gymslips. A broad window on the staircase suffused the area with light and the smell of wax polish and fresh flowers was everywhere. I noticed roses on a table near the door. Inside the hall the colour of the staircase was repeated in the polished parquet floor, patterned by sunlight from french windows along one side. There was nothing here of the worn carpets and cracked linoleum I was used to at home, nor of the grime and smell of chalk and children which pervaded St Silas'.

My first day passed in a blur of strange places and faces as we were shown round and supplied with text and exercise books by first one teacher and then another, whose names I instantly forgot. The extensive grounds had everything: landscaped grassland for games, a disused stable-yard as a playground, shrubberies for hide and seek, well-kept lawns and flowerbeds and a neglected kitchen garden. That, overhung by trees and dissected by overgrown paths and crumbling walls, reminded me of Frances Hodgson-Burnett's *Secret Garden*, though I learnt that we were to have our own patches in it to cultivate.

Though not much greater in area than St Silas', if at all, the central building with its two main floors so bright and fresh with light wood and pastel paints, contrasting with the back stairs, basements and attics, both fascinated and intimidated me. I had been put in Form IIIA3, in the care of Miss Bristow, in a room almost opposite the top of the handsome staircase, where I was pleased to find that my surname had once again placed me in my preferred position in the back corner of the room. I was upset when it became clear that Caroline and I would be in different forms, but once in my new classroom I spotted Hilary, my dancing friend, and promptly went across to her. 'All my friends are in other classes,' I announced, 'so you're going to be my friend,' and surprisingly, she was.

That administrative separation was the beginning of the end of my really close friendship with Caroline, but this time without tears or drama. By the time we left Crosshill we were drifting into becoming members of a group rather than special friends, though for a long time we continued to go about together outside school.

But that was for the future. Meanwhile, I had to adjust to my new world, at home as well as in school.

Not only was my father now a qualified teacher with a steady job in Blackburn and more regular hours, but as early as 1947 he had started studying at Blackburn Technical College in the evenings. By the time I started at the High School he had already passed both the examinations of the Union of Lancashire and Cheshire Institutes in secretarial practice and accounting, and those admitting him to membership of the Chartered Institute of Secretaries. And he did not stop there. The following year saw him back at night school classes at the Technical College, taking Royal Society of Arts examinations as well as the three A Levels which would qualify him to enrol on an external degree course at London University.

He had always studied at night, and now that I had homework as well as my brother, term-time evenings settled into a pattern of the three of us working away at the living room table once David or I had sided it after tea, depending on whose turn it was. Space dictated that this was set against the back wall, so David and I sat at opposite ends with our schoolbooks, where my parents usually sat for meals, and my father with his back to the fire occupying our usual places. David normally had the third dining chair and I my stool, which could be pushed out of the way and fitted neatly into the niche at the side of the fireplace when all four of us sat round the fire. I would have liked the fourth chair, but that was stored in the front room because there was no space for it.

For his own studies my father hammered away on a second-hand Remington typewriter which he used for the rest of his life. As I worked, the ting of its bell at the end of the lines and the grating of its carriage return merged with the sound of shifting coal, the dog snuffling in his basket or Mother rattling pots and pans in the kitchen next door. Not always though. My father spent lots of time preparing lessons, often involving me and David and sometimes my mother as well. My interest in foreign lands was born in that cramped living room as we helped him make a collage for his classroom wall about the road to Samarkand, and in his sending away for information about the American election in 1952. David was far more interested in the political aspects of that than I was, but I spent hours looking through the huge heap of colourful pamphlets and leaflets that arrived and knew rather more about the US system of government than I did about our own. Nicknamed Buck, my father had a reputation as a disciplinarian but cared about his pupils, whose Christmas presents replaced the pipes he persistently lost. He took them walking in the countryside, to play football on Saturdays and on educational visits. I often went too, and bananas figured again on one trip; golden mountains of them being unloaded on the quayside in Preston Docks.

Our evening sessions were often preceded by or included listening to the wireless. Some days I dashed home from school to listen to my favourite Children's Hour programmes including *Toy Town* and *Norman and Henry Bones: the Boy Detectives*, whose exploits I also read about. In the evenings the strains of *The Flight of the Bumble Bee* saw me and David rushing to listen to *Dick Barton, Special Agent*, or the ethereal title announcement drawing us to *Journey into Space*. My father insisted on listening to the news and *The Archers*, which my mother also followed closely. Naturally we all heard each other's favourites since the one wireless was in the living room. It was on most of the time, so I heard everything from the measured tones of Charles Hill as The Radio Doctor, discussing bowel problems as I left for school in the morning, to *Workers' Playtime* and a host of variety programmes during the holidays.

Once she had finished in the kitchen in the evenings Mother joined us and darned socks, knitted or read the paper in her chair in front of the fire, or sometimes, when we complained that she was keeping the heat from reaching us, in my father's bigger one. That, one of the armchairs from the three-piece suite which would not fit in the front room, was off to one side. In summer David went upstairs, but most of the year it was far too cold to use any other room. Though I hated the ritual of filling our stone sarsaparilla jars with boiling water every night, I never went to bed without my hot water bottle in winter, nor got dressed in the morning without first pulling my liberty bodice and knickers into the bed to warm up before going down to the fireside to put my clothes on. I liked the cat as extra warmth at night too, but unfortunately for her, so did David. She struggled frantically as we fought to pull her from one bed to the other, a bundle of soft warm fur stretched between us until finally saved by my mother's shout from below, 'Have you two got that cat upstairs again?'

'No!' we replied in unison, letting go of the poor creature, which hurtled down the stairs like a thunderbolt. Nevertheless, I often woke in the morning to find she had returned to provide me with a cosy, purring collar.

Having released the cat, David and I often resorted to word games, usually *Yes and No* in which the words had, of course, to be avoided in answering each other's questions, or *Twenty Questions*. We did our best to imitate the BBC programme, though my 'next object' did not always justify the animal, vegetable or mineral label I accorded to it, which annoyed my brother. We also used torches to read under the bedclothes, not only to avoid detection, but also because it was too cold to do anything else. Mother read to us when we were small, but never upstairs. There were fireplaces in both bedrooms but neither was used unless one of us was ill in bed for some length of time, or if the doctor recommended it.

Just as my mother had continued to use the shops she was familiar with in Victoria Street, so she had continued to use the same doctor, even though his surgery was so distant. As I grew older I thought this silly, but could hardly complain. My very earliest flicker of memory, even before that of my father returning from South Africa with the dolls and bananas, is of Dr Greeves's deep, even tones as I fought the early death from whooping cough from which he saved me. I have a hazy recollection of the fire lit then, the light on and tension in the room. I feel my weakness, the agony of the endless, all-consuming cough, and finally abandoning myself to it in much the same way that I was later to abandon myself to the murky depths of Blakey Moor Baths. Thus my objection was certainly not to the doctor himself, but to the inconvenience of the distance to his surgery. I can still see myself, one winter's evening, an unhappy victim of it.

It's already getting dark; threatening rain. My stomach ache and queasiness are far worse than when I went to school this morning so Mother has left a note for David, made me wrap up again in my school coat and scarf and we are sitting on the bus at the end of Meins Road. I'm feeling sorry for myself and huddle into the corner of the seat, giving only monosyllabic responses to her remarks as I fold my arms tightly over my stomach and stare into the bleak world outside. The engine is running, so at least the bus is warm, but it seems ages before the driver sets off, picking up few passengers on the way into town at this time of day. When we board the bus up to Bastwell it's raining, so the people who crowd on create a stifling atmosphere of damp warmth as they drip along the aisle, bags and umbrellas dangling. Fortunately it's not so full that I need to give up my seat, but I'm not sorry when we reach our stop near Belper Street Baths, and fresher air.

We've made the surgery before six so the outer door is still open. The inner one makes its familiar rattle as Mother closes it behind us. Dust and disinfectant assail my nostrils as I stand on the worn floor, searching the shabby leather benches which line the walls for a gap big enough for both of us. There isn't much room but people move up. Mother takes the space next to an old man whose laboured breathing and outbreaks of coughing sound thunderous in the stillness, leaving me to sit between her and a young, red-haired woman wearing a worn coat. She's very thin, her face is pinched and I notice that she is twisting her fingers all the time, but she returns my smile. Nobody speaks.

Heads rise as another elderly man shuffles in, briefly bringing with him the sound of voices and the swish of tyres from the wet road outside, to be cut off abruptly by the closing of the door. I note the newcomer carefully, as I shall note everyone who comes in after us to ensure that we don't miss our turn. How I hope it will be soon. It's dark outside now, and apart from an occasional splash of colour from a passing bus and the faint illumination from a single street lamp, the top panes of the frosted windows facing the road are black squares above our heads, adding to my sense of isolation in the ill-lit waiting room.

A shaft of light pierces the short corridor leading to the doctor's room as his door opens. A wizened old woman limps towards us, stick tapping, and pauses at the narrow dispensary to hand over a prescription. More frosted glass restricts my view, but I watch a shadowy figure moving about behind it and listen to the sound of drawers opening and the chink of bottles. Meanwhile a bell jangles, at which the woman next to me stands up smartly and clicks down the corridor into the consulting room. The old crone leaves and once more we all stare blankly at the ground. The pain is worse and I want to talk to my mother but feel too oppressed even to whisper, as people come and go. At six o'clock the shadowy figure is revealed as the white-coated wife of the doctor, as she strides across the room to lock the outside door. As she disappears again someone bangs on it and rattles the handle, but too late. The door remains locked.

Eventually the bell clangs for us and our footsteps echo on the two or three yards of worn linoleum leading to the doctor's door. It slopes down slightly, something I never remember and can't see in the gloom, so my feet slap down hard as I find the ground not quite where I expect it. Mother taps on the door before pushing it fully open. 'Come in. Sit down,' Dr Greeves rumbles, and I perch on a chair next to her, in front of the massive desk which takes up about a third of the cluttered room. I'm nervous now, even though I know and like him and his gruff geniality.

'So what's the problem today?' he asks, after a word or two with my mother about the family which I don't take in. She tells him about my pain so he turns to me and hesitantly I explain. Extricating himself from the desk, he prods me. 'Where does it hurt? There? There?'

I think he's found the area, so I say 'Yes.' He looks thoughtful for a moment before returning to his seat to write out a prescription which he hands to my mother. And that's it. At least there's no saying 'Aah' today, or suffering his cold stethoscope. Now it's our turn to pause at the dispensary where I'm pleased to see that my medicine is no more than the customary pink, chalky mixture which tastes quite pleasant and seems to cure me, though the visit to get it doesn't seem to be doing me much good. All I want now is to be at home in bed, cuddling a hot water bottle to counter the cold of the bedroom, and it's still two uncomfortable bus rides away.

It was the perpetual cold in the house that finally drove my parents to give up attempting to wrest improvements from the landlord and settle for his consent to changes. Some years later, when the back boiler died of old age, they replaced it themselves, put a modern tiled fireplace in the living room and had a radiator installed on the system in the back bedroom that David and I shared. The removal of the range meant no side oven for warming plates and melting butter, but since it also meant extra heating and no more black leading no one minded

– except perhaps the cat, who lost her special snoozing spot in the top oven. After that, as long as the fire was alight, we had the luxury of regular heating in two rooms in addition to the trusty one-bar electric fire which Mother kept in the kitchen. I never pined for Jack Frost's icy pictures on the inside of the bedroom windows in winter, attractive though they were.

Having heating in the bedroom more or less coincided with my beginning the nights in my parents' bed and being moved to my own when they came upstairs. That way David could stay up later without keeping me awake and pursue his own interests, largely reading, making things and listening to music. Having failed in his efforts to build himself a crystal set, he saved up for a transistor radio and, to my chagrin since I was not there to hear it, went to sleep listening to Radio Luxembourg. Meanwhile, I was coming to terms with my new school environment.

Blackburn High School had a wide social mix, more so perhaps than my junior school, which drew almost exclusively from the parish in which it stood. Four single-sex grammar schools, two of them Roman Catholic and two, including mine, non-denominational, served the whole town with its population of around 100,000. Though the boys' grammar school, Queen Elizabeth's, also took private pupils, our school did not. Thus the only aspects we new arrivals had in common were the ability to pass the exam and the uniforms we wore. My new companions ranged from the daughters of professional people to those from council estates where the residents were reputed to use their gates and fences for fuel and keep their coal in the bath. Identically clad, they all seemed much the same to me.

In retrospect it appears to me that the aim of the school was to take its socially diverse assortment of little girls, shake them up and empty them out of the box as young ladies with a good, all-round education, able and willing to make the best of their various talents. That sounds fine, but the stress seemed to be on the production of young ladies, and that was where I began to fall foul of authority, despite my desire to please.

Fighting with Hilary was one of my first offences. This was an amicable, pre-arranged contest, billed to take place in the stable yard one dinner time with an audience of our classmates to cheer us on. I was baffled when we were stopped by a prefect and hauled off to the duty mistress for an inquisition. She was a charismatic and voluble lady with a rather plummy accent whom I chiefly remember for leaping about at the front of the classroom pretending to be a signpost while declaring, in carefully enunciated tones 'This, that, these, those, are demonstrative pronouns.' On this occasion, however, she seemed strangely restrained. Having failed to find a quarrel she could sort out she contented herself with a brief reprimand in which she reminded us that little girls did not fight –

which was a completely new concept for me – and told us we must never do so again. My next offence was far more complicated.

'Quiet, now,' came the expected command from a young teacher whose name I had yet to learn, rising over the babble of sound from the dining tables which gradually died away. It was the beginning of the silent period between courses, and we did not obey fast enough to suit her. 'Quiet!' she reiterated more loudly. 'I said quiet!' Hilary and I exchanged glances and smiled. 'You two, you heard what I said. Stand up!' She was looking straight at us. I could not believe it at first, but there was no mistake. 'The red-head, and you, with the fringe.' Slowly, hot with embarrassment and seeing Hilary's face turn almost the same colour as her hair as she joined me, I pushed back my chair and stood up, the two of us the focus of every pair of eyes in the now silent dining room.

'But, but we weren't talking,' Hilary began, tears beginning to form. To tell the truth she cried very easily, so much so that we used to tease her to make her cry just for the fun of it, but on this occasion, I was close to tears myself.

'Don't lie to me. Of course you were. I'm putting you both in detention. Now sit down.'

I was distraught; detention, the ultimate punishment. Even if I could manage to conceal it from my parents I knew it would appear on my report, and I had not done anything wrong. Sinking back into my chair I pushed my pudding aside in my misery, but Hilary was less easily defeated.

'I'm going to complain,' she declared, as soon as we were allowed to talk again. 'I'm going to tell Miss Bristow and you're coming with me.' Dismally I followed her to the staffroom at the beginning of afternoon school to waylay our form-mistress, comforting myself with the thought that we could not make things worse. To my surprise, Hilary was given a hearing and the detention rescinded in favour of a lecture on attitude, though from her subsequent behaviour towards me I always felt that the younger mistress neither forgot nor forgave. The injustice rankled with me and was eventually to influence my attitude to my own pupils.

The one real detention I served at Crosshill I had no complaints about. Any first year who had the temerity, or perhaps I should say the idiocy, to read a novel under her desk in one of Mrs Scholick's maths lessons deserved everything she got. I wonder now what book it was that drove me to be so careless of consequences; perhaps *Pride and Prejudice,* one of our early reading books which left me hungry for more. Mrs Scholick, as innocent of any hint of physical violence as all my secondary school teachers and beloved by senior girls was, in her biting strictness towards juniors, Crosshill's nearest approximation to Miss Middleton. Forget to put the date at the top of the page, fail to rule a line under a heading or, horror of horrors, knock a pencil or ruler off your desk into the silence of her lesson and you were in for verbal massacre, delivered in her distinctive, grating voice. Thus what I really learnt from her was not so much mathematics, but the virtue of being careful, accurate and well-behaved. It was lucky that geometry at that level was largely drawing, which I was good at. Even though she was more tolerant of lack of ability than she was of behaviour that fell below her standards, I was too frightened to ask questions.

A further lesson in behaviour derived from an incident involving the headmistress, Miss Ormerod, normally a remote being far above dealing with our minor misdemeanours, whose ever-open door we tiptoed past to avoid notice. Nevertheless she commanded both liking and respect, and was a person whose good opinion I truly valued. Thus I was mortified when I found myself about to lose it.

'Go on,' Hilary urged me. 'I dare you!' It was cold and dismal outside. We had sneaked into the building at dinner time and were hiding close to the kitchen entrance, ready to make a speedy exit if spotted. 'Go on,' Hilary whispered again. 'Run to the corner and back.' I listened. Nothing. I eyed up the distance, then ran – and came nose to waist with Miss Ormerod as she rounded the corner. A stately lady, hair scraped back above florid features, cameo at her throat, brown woollen dress above lisle stockings and brogues, she towered above me as I skidded to a halt, horribly conscious of my outdoor shoes scuffing the polished parquet.

'Joan,' she rumbled into the silence, 'What are you doing inside? Why are you running? Is something the matter?' Shocked and scared I broke every code I knew – home, school, Brownies, Enid Blyton, everything – and for the first and last time in my life, attempted to lie my way out of trouble.

'No, Miss Ormerod. I came in to get my handkerchief.'

'Your handkerchief? Surely that would be in your coat pocket. This is not the way to the cloakroom.' Committed now, I lied again.

'Please, Miss Ormerod, it's in my desk.'

'I see. Then let us both go and find it.'

Obviously she did see – right through me – so my march to the guillotine began. Stomach churning, achingly aware of ordinary sounds: shouts from outside; a piano playing somewhere in the building and, closer, the soft click of a latch as Hilary made her escape, I followed her along the corridor, sick with shame and fear. What would she think of me? What would she do? Would she tell my father? I swallowed hard. Up the staircase we proceeded, across the landing and into the classroom, our footfalls drumbeats in the emptiness.

'Which desk?' Legs trembling, I led the way to the back corner, raised my desk lid with a clammy hand, cringing as it squealed into the silence, and waited for the axe to fall.

'Put it in your pocket quickly, and go back…'

I hardly heard the rest as I stared, in stunned relief, at the grubby handkerchief which lay on top of my books.

Shortly after that I opted for dinner time fresh air on my own terms, walking home for my mother's company and cooking and a seat by the fire. In so doing I inadvertently became a shopper for my schoolfellows because no one who did stay for dinner was allowed off the premises. Every afternoon, when I returned, I found a small gathering at the end of the drive waiting to give me money to make purchases for them from the small shop in Manor Road. David said I should charge them for the service, or at least insist on being given some of the goods – he would have done. The shop was only about 20 yards from the gate but no one was prepared to risk going out. Mrs Scholick lived between the two.

Though I jibbed at the world of rules and regulations I had moved into, they were always outweighed by the wealth of new experiences which awaited me. Among these was music. Though I had chorused away happily in Miggy's classes, being a girl I had been forbidden the church choir. Now I found that I could join the school's junior choir provided that I could pass an audition. Happily, my nervously quavering rendition of *The Ash Grove* proved adequate and a member I became, with all the attendant pleasures of the singing itself and membership of a dedicated group. In addition, there were instrumental lessons.

I, whose last contact with a musical instrument had been to thump and shake a tambourine and tap a triangle in the babies' class at three years old, was to learn to play the recorder. I was filled with happy anticipation, only to be sadly disappointed as I discovered that I did not, and indeed do not, like the sound. Soon I played only under duress and complained perpetually. Relief came when my mother found that I could have additional free lessons on other instruments, retrieved her long-neglected violin from its resting place under the stairs and provided me with something I could enjoy.

I also enjoyed just being in the music room, so able to admire the intricate plasterwork, particularly the ceiling rose, delicately picked out in pale blue and white to match the pastel colours of the building's interior. I had seen nothing like it before and thought it incredibly beautiful. Not only that, but french windows opened from both it and the adjacent hall, once the ballroom, onto a shallow flight of steps leading down to the shrubbery-encircled formal lawns and flowerbeds. Wordsworth had his inner vision of daffodils – mine is of that garden one sunlit, summer afternoon; not so much for the scent and colour of flowers alone, but for the whole experience, epitomised by the exquisite sound of a harp, being played for us by a former pupil to a background of birdsong and the murmur of insects.

My interest in buildings having been awakened, at the other extreme I also noticed the features of the sickroom on the one miserable afternoon I spent there. It was Easter, and for some reason we had all been given chocolate eggs that morning. I, having taken mine home, returned to school to find an investigation in progress because an egg had been stolen. I was shocked, but when told to sit down and read I soon lost interest, and hardly noticed as one or two girls were summoned for interview. This time I know the book that gripped me. It was *Prester John*, a novel which delighted me with both story and setting and led me to read every John Buchan I could find. Before long, however, I was distracted by feeling so sick that I put my hand up and told Mrs Johnson.

I was immediately despatched to sit in the sickroom with a bucket to hand and nothing to do but look around me and think. I found I was in a narrow bathroom, quite small, but with a very lofty ceiling and illuminated by just one high window. It contained a large, ornate wash basin and lavatory, the latter on a raised platform I seem to remember, and crammed between them and the bath, a chair and a camp-bed for casualties. The real feature was the bath. It was strange, and oddly unnerving. I could see no curved underside or iron claw feet as I could with our bath, because it was boxed into one long wall with the same heavy, dark wood as the dado which decorated the other walls, quite different from the woodwork in the public areas. But what really distinguished it was a screen. This was a panel in the same wood, the full length of the alcove and perhaps twice the height of the bath itself, which clearly went up and down like a sash window. It was slightly raised, so I could see there was no one there, but it both repelled and fascinated me.

I have since searched in vain for its like, though at the time it, my sickness and the whole dismal aspect of the room did nothing for my state of mind. I suddenly saw, with a terrible clarity, that an egg had disappeared, I was sick and it would be assumed that I had stolen it and eaten it. Scared as well as ill, I sat there for the rest of the afternoon hoping desperately that the culprit would be found; fearing every footstep in the corridor was the preface to an accusation. I was not reassured when the thief was never identified, even though the offence was considered so serious that Miss Ormerod took charge of the investigation herself.

Miss Ormerod's involvement in anything was always significant, and slightly earlier that same year her tears had introduced me to a type and depth of adult grief which I had never been allowed to share at home. Even on this occasion, it manifested itself in my presence only in sad silence. It was 6 February, Hilary's 12th birthday, and to celebrate it she had been allowed to invite some of us to go to the pictures with her. That was something to look forward to in itself, but the real thrill was that we were to go on our own, without her parents. What an escapade it promised to be. As a result we were especially excited that morning and completely untroubled as we filed downstairs for an unexpected assembly – until Miss Ormerod walked in, red-eyed and blowing her nose. We were already in fidgety silence, but the stillness in the hall became palpable, her sniffling quite audible. I felt tense, almost afraid. This was completely out of character. What was coming?

'Colleagues, girls,' she began, 'I'm afraid I have to tell you.' She paused, obviously unable to continue, then tried again. 'I have to tell you that His Majesty, King George VI, has passed away. You are to return to your form rooms and prepare to go home.' She departed as abruptly as she had arrived, back straight, head up, though weeping, a model of dignified grief.

Although affected by the atmosphere, I was mainly bewildered. The King meant nothing to me. I had seen his picture on stamps but that was about all, and Hilary and I were more concerned with her birthday celebrations. We agreed to meet as planned, not having understood the import of what we had heard. I was lucky in living close to school. By the time Hilary left for home the buses had stopped running so she had to walk the three miles to Ramsgreave Drive. Shops and mills closed early, cinemas never opened and BBC programmes gave way to martial music as Blackburn, in tune with the rest of the nation, went into sombre mourning for the much loved and respected monarch who had shared his people's wartime agonies.

The death of the King resulted in memorial services up and down the country, including one in St Silas' Church. Its attendant parade naturally involved the Guides, of which by that time I was one. Recognising the solemnity of the occasion we marched there in silence, handed over our flags and took up our places in the front pew with due decorum, but it was not to last. As the Revd Gordon Walker intoned his eulogy, Caroline nudged me and nodded towards the foot of the pulpit. Thereafter, as the congregation behind us sat in sorrowful and respectful silence, some surreptitiously weeping, we fought to control our giggles at the antics of a mouse which was running about near the chancel steps, sometimes coming closer to us and sometimes pausing to look up warily as the volume of the vicar's voice increased. More and more grins appeared as our companions traced the source of our mirth but fortunately, assisted by scowls from both Scout and Guide leaders, we managed to contain ourselves until we were outside.

Incidents and Excursions

When the time came I had opted to join St Silas' Guides, even though the High School boasted two Guide companies, the 9th and the 59th. It was possibly the first serious decision I had to make. Prior to that I had simply drifted where my parents or events directed me, and choosing was not easy. Consulting my friends, I found that some were joining one company, some another and others none at all; consulting my mother and father I was encouraged to consider the advantages and disadvantages and make up my own mind.

I had enjoyed both St Silas' School and its Brownies and did not want to lose contact with the boys and girls I had known for so long, who were of different ages and in some cases attended, or would be attending, different schools. At the same time I knew that the High School companies were more active and progressive and, above all, went camping, as David had done with the Scouts. Whatever I did I would not be mixing with him, since he had left to join the Air Training Corps in furtherance of his desire for a career in the RAF.

So was it to be fun with established friends in the outside world or more guided guiding in a more confined community? I settled on the former, a decision I never regretted. Thus it was that shortly after my introduction to secondary school I left the Brownies' Fairy Ring for the last time to 'fly up' to Guides with some of my friends by stepping over the clasped hands of two lines of those we were leaving behind. Brown Owl said nice things about us and wished us well, but I felt quite sad as it came home to me that it was an end as much as a beginning. I had not felt that at all about the school, having been far too excited about what was to come.

Being in the Guides, without the extra dimension of camping, was in many ways little more than an extension of Brownies with very similar tests to be passed and badges earned, but I appreciated the social differences. Rather than being concert performers, in conjunction with the Scouts we became workers at money-raising events from which we derived just as much pleasure in that we were out and about doing things as a group. One of these, the Vicarage Garden Party, was an annual event that I looked forward to with particular anticipation, even though it meant not much more than an afternoon of party food, apple bobbing, lucky dip and organised games – and helping to clear up afterwards. The one year that it was for some reason held in the grounds of Westholme, the small, private preparatory school across the road with which we St Silas' pupils had a running feud similar to that with Sacred Heart, I think we also had pony rides. There was a stable behind Westholme where Christine sometimes went riding, which regularly provided ponies for the far more elaborate Liberal Party garden parties she and I attended with our parents over the years, at 'Rockwood' on Billinge End Road, near Heathfield Convent on Meins Road, and even at Salmesbury Hall and Riley Green.

I remember only one Guide concert and that, I am sorry to say, because of the extreme embarrassment it caused me. A fellow Guide, Marjorie, who was also learning to play the violin, volunteered the two of us to play a duet. I was appalled. Being well aware of my own incompetence but unable to extricate myself I could only practise desperately. On the appointed night we took up our positions, backs to the window, facing an audience of parents and church supporters about 3ft from us. There was no curtain, no protective platform, no dimmed lights as there had always been for dancing – just them and us. Trying to avoid looking at their encouraging and expectant faces I adjusted the position of my violin with a trembling hand and we began to scrape away in unison at a simple tune. It was fine at first and I began to relax, but too soon. We failed to keep together and, as we gradually lost our unity, Marjorie trailed into silence leaving me to play on my own, hearing my uncertain notes quavering agonisingly into the now uncomfortable stillness. She tried to pick up the tune again, failed, and fled into the kitchen. I played a few more painful bars, gave up and ran after her.

Far more fun were general activities such as bring and buy sales in the Parish Rooms, and the socials there that my father at last considered me old enough to attend alone. I had to be collected from them though, a task frequently delegated to David along with his regular job of collecting me from the Guide meetings in school on Fridays. We both hated it; he because he had to turn out in all weathers and then trail through the streets with his little sister, me because I wanted to hang about the chip shop in New Bank Road with my friends. I used to bribe his silence with half my occasional threepennyworth of chips, but we still walked home in mutinous silence at opposite sides of the pavement.

Being a Guide also gave me the opportunity to get close to the Queen, or at least to her car, when she visited Blackburn during the tour of the country she made following the Coronation. Despite the rain, flags and bunting fluttered aloft and the streets were packed with cheering crowds. The atmosphere was tremendous, but best of all, the various youth organisations lined the route in front of the crowd. I felt so proud, standing to attention on King William Street in my specially pressed uniform as the Queen drove slowly past a few feet from me. Once she was inside the Town Hall and we were dismissed, Caroline and I ran all the way to Bastwell to see her again and wave as she went by. She waved back and made our day complete.

Despite enjoying the other Guide activities I never lost my desire to go camping. The problem was that our Captain did not have the necessary licence, so though we went out into the countryside to learn and practise camping skills, including erecting tents, lighting fires and cooking, and sometimes stayed out late to sing round the embers at dusk, in the end we always had to go home. As a result, most of my fireside singing took place in Youth Hostel common rooms.

My very first Youth Hostelling trip was to Kettlewell, in the Yorkshire Dales, with my parents and a small group from the Rambling Club. It was 1951 or 1952, and certainly Easter as we bought warm hot cross buns from a baker's van in a village somewhere, so it must have been Good Friday, the only day in the year they were available. Also, I was surprised by the walk beginning late on Sunday because virtually everyone in the group expected to go to church. It was snowing, and since the hostel was locked as normal between 10am and 5pm, we went along with the others as somewhere warm to wait, if nothing else.

It was glorious during the day, walking the hills in sunlit snow, but desperately cold at night, even colder in the hostel than it normally was at home. After a hot evening meal followed by a session of singing and talking round the single blazing fire, we went to our narrow bunks to huddle in thin, cotton sleeping bags under a couple of rough blankets topped with all our clothes, and still shivered. I woke in the morning to ice on the sheet where my breath had frozen during the night. I was used to ice on the inside of window panes, but not that. However, I was enjoying myself too much to care.

I soon learnt how to achieve two layers beneath me and four on top with just two blankets, and did not even mind the jobs we all had to do in the morning. Somehow, helping with the washing up or sweeping the dormitory floor seemed far less onerous than such tasks did at home, where David and I took turns each week to clean either the living room or the stairs and passage. The only cleaning I liked was polishing, but unless we did a proper job with everything, there was no pocket money. I particularly loathed grovelling under the sideboard with the duster mop, and it was even worse trying to do it with the Ewbank when we eventually replaced the linoleum and carpet square with a red patterned fitted carpet. Even so, I loved the carpet, which we all went to choose. I remember rolling on the thick pile like a puppy before the furniture was replaced.

As soon as we returned from our YHA trip I wanted to go again, so my parents decided that in the summer they would take me once more, together with some of my friends. In the end we went for at least three years in succession, not always quite the same group of girls, but always to the Yorkshire Dales, easily accessible by train from Blackburn to Hellifield. My mother and father took us first, then my mother with a friend's mother, and finally a teacher, Miss Hartley, who used the trip to start a school YHA group. Though the first excursions were unofficial, one of them, in 1953 at the end of my second and final year at Crosshill, was written up in the school magazine. Apparently we were named best school party of the year at Kettlewell, something not entirely consistent with the report, which not only mentions girls falling off stepping stones into the River Wharf at Linton in Craven and someone losing a shoe in a bog, but also a nose-bleed resulting from a pillow fight.

I forget now the order in which we visited the villages, or what happened when, but some incidents stand out from the overall pleasure I derived from being out in glorious countryside with my friends, walking happily from hostel to hostel as the rules then required – unless you happened to be travelling by bicycle or canoe. I found two events which took place at Malham Hostel far from enjoyable. The first was fairly minor and basically beneficial, though I was overcome by shame at the time. We had already been away for a night or so, enjoying, or so I thought, convivial meals at long tables, when Caroline took me on one side. She wanted to tell me to stop chewing with my mouth open because everyone was sick of it. It took me a long time to recover from that shock, but even longer to recover from the other incident which occurred when my father was with us.

Caroline and I had gone out together before the evening meal to explore the village. It was quite small and before long we had exhausted its possibilities and so, on a lovely summer's evening, we found ourselves playing in the river by Beck Hall, where we were joined by two slightly older boys who were also staying at the hostel. In due course, almost late for our meal, the four of us returned to the hostel together. There I was stunned to find my father on the doorstep, beside himself with anger. The others slid past as he grabbed me.

'Where've you been? What d'you think you're playing at?' he demanded, giving me no chance to reply. 'I won't have you going out with strange boys. You don't know them, where they're from, anything,' and with that he smacked me across the face with such force that I staggered into the hall. Now it was my turn to shout. He had never hit me like that before, and I was shocked into unwonted retaliation.

'How could you?' I raged. 'And in front of my friends, and everybody. I hate you! I hate you! I'm not going home. I'm going to stay here for ever.' On I went, shouting, sobbing, saying anything that came into my head, more and more incoherent, displaying a temper equal to his own, and finally fleeing in tears to the blessedly empty, female dormitory, where he could not follow.

For the rest of the evening I refused to go anywhere near him, including down to supper, even to please my mother who came to find me. I could not have eaten anyway, my outburst having left me so sick and with such a hammering headache.

Me, my mother, my brother and my father at the top of the front garden in 1940, the year I was born.

An RAF camp near Durban, South Africa, in 1942. My father is on the left.

The photograph of me, complete with name and troopship cabin number on the back, which my father carried off to war with him.

The Memorial Garden near the entrance to Corporation Park.

The Market Hall and the top of the market with some of the temporary stalls, probably viewed from Booth's café.

Renewing my father's acquaintance during the war.

Cadgwith's shingle fishing beach.

My navigator father with his pilot, Eric Kimber, and their Mosquito.

My uncle, Herbert Ryan, killed in action in 1945 aged 19.

My grandfather's shop at No. 123 Victoria Street.

Our front garden as it always was in spring.

Billinge Scar, the ruin where we found the swimming pool, as it was in its 19th-century hey-day as the home of first the Thwaites and then the Birtwistle family. (© *Blackburn with Darwen Library and Information Services*)

Our front door and my route to the roof, covered in winter snow.

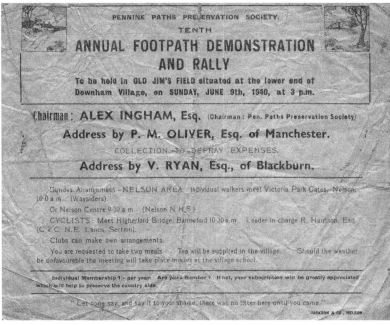

PENNINE PATHS PRESERVATION SOCIETY.

TENTH

ANNUAL FOOTPATH DEMONSTRATION
AND RALLY

To be held in OLD JIM'S FIELD situated at the lower end of
Downham Village, on SUNDAY, JUNE 9th, 1940, at 3 p.m.

Chairman: **ALEX INGHAM, Esq.** (Chairman: Pen. Paths Preservation Society)

Address by P. M. OLIVER, Esq. of Manchester.

COLLECTION TO DEFRAY EXPENSES.

Address by V. RYAN, Esq., of Blackburn.

Sunday Arrangement—NELSON AREA Individual walkers meet Victoria Park Gates, Nelson,
10-0 a.m. (Waysiders).

Or Nelson Centre 9-30 a.m. (Nelson N.H.S.)

CYCLISTS: Meet Higherford Bridge, Barrowford 10-30 a.m. Leader in charge R. Harrison, Esq.
(C.T.C. N.E. Lancs. Section).

Clubs can make own arrangements.

You are requested to take two meals. Tea will be supplied in the village. Should the weather
be unfavourable the meeting will take place indoors at the village school.

Individual Membership 1/- per year. Are you a member? If not, your subscription will be greatly appreciated
which will help to preserve the country side.

"Let none say, and say it to your shame, there was no litter here until you came."

JACKSON & CO., NELSON.

Notice of the local footpath preservation society rally at which my father spoke.

My mother, wearing the brown, corduroy shorts I inherited which, before she was married, she had to conceal from her father and change into outside town when she went rambling.

Posing at Edisford Bridge, my father at the back of the group, me on the left and my new step-uncle, John Dixon, on the right.

The cast of a Rambling Club pantomime, including me on the left.

Out with my extended family of ramblers, my mother on the wall on the right behind my father and the dog, David and me in the centre.

Some of the makers of the film *Then Came Isobel* and their families, but not the cast.

Saving the cat from snow in Whinfield's drive. David, aged 13, is wearing his Technical High School uniform.

St Silas' Church and Parish Rooms.

St Silas's Brownies c.1948, me holding the staff, Caroline second from the left on the back row and Betty at the right-hand end.

In third place behind Mr Briggs, the school caretaker, with Caroline behind me, in the line up for a Whit Walk near Leamington Road Church.

Merrie England in Corporation Park. (*Northern Daily Telegraph*, 10 August 1951)

The official send-off on the Town Hall steps for the Beating of the Bounds.

Following the town boundary across the Leeds and Liverpool canal somewhere near Whitebirk.

We, the members of the Blackburn Rambling Association who have subscribed our names hereby testify that on the eleventh day of August, one thousand ninehundred and fifty-one, the Boundaries of the County Borough as shown on this plan were duly perambulated as part of the Celebrations comme-morating the Centenary of the Incorporation of the Borough.

1. Joan Mary Ryan.
2. Alan John Ainsworth.
3. Christine Howarth.
4. David Victor Ryan
5. Edward Geo Billington
6. Hilda Billington
7. W J Britchley
8. James Hargreaves.
9. Elsie Hargreaves.
10. William Edgar Holburt.
11. Edith M. Holden.
12. Arnold Hornby
13. Elsie Hornby
14. Victor Ryan
15. Doris Ryan
16. Edith Shaw
17. Leonard Shaw.
18. Alan Shorrock
19. Robt. Taylor.
20. Rebecca Taylor.
21. T W Inkley

The official declaration signed by those who walked Blackburn's entire 1851 boundary.

Crosshill, home of Blackburn High School junior department. *(courtesy of Barbara Riding)*

Miss Hartley's YHA party, Enid next to me at the right-hand side and Marjorie in front.

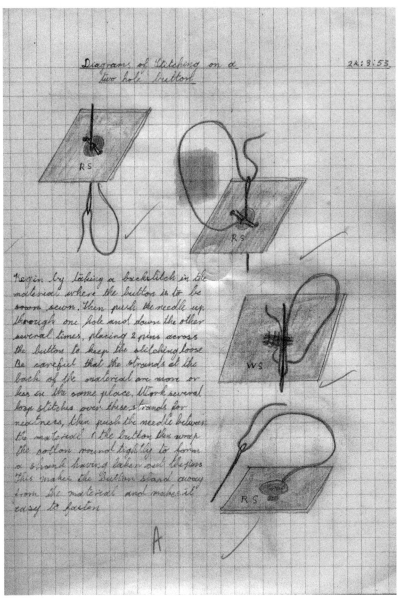

Diagrams of Stitching on a
Two hole button

2A: 3·53

R.S

R.S

W.S

R.S

Begin by taking a backstitch in the
material where the button is to be
sewn sewn. Then push the needle up
through one hole and down the other
several times, placing 2 pins across
the button to keep the stitching loose.
Be careful that the strands at the
back of the material are more or
less in the same place. Work several
loop stitches over these strands for
neatness, then push the needle between
the material & the button then wrap
the cotton round tightly to form
a strand having taken out the pins.
This makes the button stand away
from the material and makes it
easy to fasten

A

A sample of the needlework course at Blackburn High School in 1953.

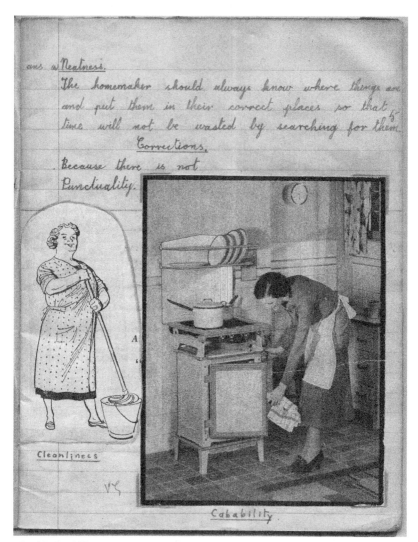

ans a) Neatness.
  The homemaker should always know where things are
  and put them in their correct places so that
  time will not be wasted by searching for them
          Corrections.
  Because there is not
  Punctuality.

Cleanliness

Cabability.

The kind of illustration required to support each topic in a domestic science note book.

Blackburn High School main building on Preston New Road. *(Courtesy of Hazel Pidcock)*

Me on the left, performing in one of the many dancing displays in which I took part.

David in ATC uniform with the shed across the back of our house visible behind him.

My father, Aunty Mary, Uncle Frank and my cousins Peter and Michael in the snow in Houghton.

Off to the beach in 1955 with my father and our Minehead landlady's daughters.

Arnside Tower, when it was still safe to climb, with Alan and me on top.

Christine riding Cracker in West Leigh Road.

Celebrating the end of term and O Levels with Enid in Southport in 1956.

With two of our group in front of the Chalet des Alpes, an annexe to the Hotel Jolimont in Les Marecottes, where I and others of the group slept.

The lower sixth skiing foursome.

The Geography sixth in Borrowdale with Miss Barker and Miss Seed, Hazel back left behind me.

Mr Bell's group on Helvellyn.

At Mr Bell's feet on Scafell Pike, with Hazel in the foreground.

Grange seafront.

My parents outside our accommodation on our final family visit to Grange.

Blackburn High School Upper Sixth, 1958, with me sixth from the left on the back row.

My father painting over the rust on his new car in the shadow of the shed.

Ready to return to Sheffield for my second year on the scooter I bought with my OTC pay.

'He didn't intend to hit you, love,' Mother said gently, as she administered aspirins and a drink. He was terribly worried when you were missing at supper time, and when you turned up with two strange boys he saw red. It's because he cares about you and wants to keep you safe.'

'But we were only playing by the river. He just hit me and made me look stupid, and it hurt.'

'I know,' she said, 'I know, but fathers worry about these things. He's just as upset about it as you are.' I was not inclined to credit that.

'But he didn't have to hit me. He didn't give me a chance to explain,' I sobbed, burying my face in the pillow of the bottom bunk where I had curled up in my misery. She tried again, but I would not be comforted, whatever she said. Eventually she sighed and left. Everyone was very quiet in the dormitory that night. What, if anything, Caroline reported to the others I do not know. She never said a word about it to me, for which I was extremely grateful, and my father and I reached an uneasy peace in the morning. He went on shouting at me when I annoyed him, but never hit me again. Nor did he accompany us on any more trips.

The third incident, also shared with Caroline, had nothing distressing about it. We had moved on to Ingleton where there was a small, open-air swimming pool at the bottom of the garden, alongside the river. Hot and sticky from walking, most of us plunged into it when we arrived and she and I thought it would be fun to get up before breakfast and go in again. Accordingly, before anyone else was about, clad in swimming costumes we padded out into the morning sunshine and jumped straight in. We emerged as two shivering wrecks.

Pursued by gales of laughter from the Warden, who was watching us from the kitchen, we rushed off to get dressed, but as a result of the escapade my father changed our plans for the day. The Warden told him that the river was threatening to undercut the pool's foundations and though some work had been done, he was going to spend the day strengthening the defensive wall by placing rocks to protect it. We exchanged a day's hike for a short walk round Ingleton waterfalls followed by a strenuous paddle in hot sun as we shifted water-smoothed grey and pink boulders around in the clear water. It was great fun – like damming streams on a massive scale – and whether we were useful that day or not, Ingleton still has its swimming pool – now heated.

Hostelling might have been new to me in 1951, but visiting the Yorkshire Dales was not. Most Rambling Club walks were local, but the Club also travelled further afield. Though I loved the sense of space and freedom on the moors around our town, I much preferred the short, green turf of the Dales with its lattice of white walls and stretches of limestone pavement, to the muddy field paths we walked on close to home. Even so, I think the turning from the main road to Hellifield station, often taken in darkness at a desperate trot after a tiring day out, is the longest half-mile I have ever endured. But I loved the railway, thrilling to the roar and hiss of its massive engines, the gleam of their metalwork and the latent power I sensed as the mighty wheels and rods propelled the monsters into motion. There was pleasure, too, in sitting by a waiting-room fire on the way home on a dark winter's night, soothed by its warmth and the crackling coals, flushed and sleepy from a day on the hills. I particularly liked one station we frequented, I forget now which, where the soft glow and gentle hiss of a gas light contributed to the cosiness of the shabby room.

Much less pleasant for me were the club's annual outings to more distant places. Walks were part of the programme, but numerous non-walking relatives and members who were no longer active also went along, and there was usually a meal in a café. I enjoyed the different destinations, but not the journeys there by chara, the abbreviation for charabanc generally used for the Robinsons, Yelloway or Weardens motor coaches we travelled on.

Though I was rarely physically sick, on roads I suffered badly from travel sickness, a problem exacerbated by my father's conviction that it was a purely imaginary malady and so at worse a source of his irritation and at best something to be ignored. I usually slept on the way back, but unless I could I sit at the front, the journey there was often misery. My more sympathetic mother tried to ensure that we were waiting in Railway Road well before departure time in order to get good seats. Nevertheless, despite the difficulties, once my father was back from the war, even as a small child I was able to enjoy the paths and landscapes of areas far beyond the boundaries of Blackburn as a result of both Rambling Club outings and our own excursions.

Closer to home, the bigger second-hand bike I had been given for passing the scholarship exam had widened the scope of my activities, making it less effort for outings such as going with Caroline to gather bluebells from the wood at the end of Meins Road. Not that I needed to, since we had a garden full, but then the fact that we grew daffodils never stopped me and David from going every year to a field near Salmesbury Bottoms where the farmer let us gather wild ones for our mother. She loved daffodils and was always pleased with our huge bunches of the small flowers. She also liked the posy of violets and primroses I bought for her on Mothering Sunday from the flower seller at the foot of the Market Hall steps. She used to tell me not to buy them because he put his prices up for the weekend from something like fourpence to sixpence, but I always did.

Not only did I cycle off with Caroline, David or Christine (before she began to prefer horses to bicycles), but also with David and my father. Once he had school holidays he took us all out, though David frequently went under sufferance because my father thought he needed some fresh air and exercise.

Once or twice we made it to Clitheroe to see Grandad, but when Uncle Frank lived in Houghton, close to Stanley Grange Police College where he was an instructor, that was frequently our destination. My mother, who could not ride a bike, lived in perpetual fear that one or other of us would be killed on the road. We never left without 'Be careful. Watch out for motor cars!' ringing in our ears. The day I had a puncture my father could not mend, so we left our bikes behind a barn and walked home, she was frantic with worry by the time we arrived.

On my own I went no further than Christine's or Hilary's, and often just to the end of Meins Road and back as I had always done, first on the tricycle I inherited from David and then on my small two-wheeler, always failing in my many attempts to make the cat stay in the bike basket as I did so. On one of these short trips I was stopped close to Preston New Road by a young foreign woman looking for Woodgate Road, which I knew was a turning about half a mile away. Since she was struggling with two suitcases and I was doing nothing in particular, I balanced the heavier case on my bike and walked back with her and up the unmade track to the house where she was going to look after the children. Observing that it was a big house with a car parked outside I thought the people must not have known when she was arriving, but my mother's view was less charitable. When I reached the stage of looking for holiday jobs, I never considered being an au pair.

I also still traversed the neighbourhood on foot, often carrying a sketchbook and stopping to draw anything which took my fancy. While studying at the Technical College my father had noticed that there were free art classes for children on Saturday mornings, and offered to enrol me. The tutor, Mr Bain, was kind and helpful, and the classes were wonderful. They offered far more scope than I had at Crosshill in introducing me to such diverse skills as block printing, throwing pots and handloom weaving, thus allowing me to clutter the house with strange patterns, wonky pots and uneven scarves and runners, of which I was inordinately proud. Because the college trained people for the cotton industry there was a small weaving shed in the basement which we were also shown, the nearest I ever got to the deafening racket of a mill, but what I really loved, after years of trying to teach myself from books, was being taught to draw.

The classes were held indoors, but they inspired me to go out and draw real places and people, with some success in that I achieved a commendation at the Agricultural Show for a drawing of Beardwood Hall, done from my perch on the roots of a tree in the grounds where I should not, of course, have been. It was as I set out along Meins Road one day, planning to do some drawing, that I met, and was frightened by, an acquaintance of my father's. Naturally I had been brought up to be wary of strange men, although I did not actually know why, and this man was no stranger. However, the tone of his voice when he offered to turn back and walk along with me was enough to make me decline and race back home. Uncertain as to whether I had been sensible or simply offended a friend of my father's, I never told anyone, though I did tell my parents about another of his friends who made me feel terribly grown up and pleased with myself by raising his hat to me one day as I was going to school.

Though I was still roaming the neighbourhood on foot and by bike, apart from excursions which had a purpose, such as the gathering of daffodils, David was no longer my regular companion and had grown out of leading me into mischief. In the holidays he went off with friends I only knew by sight, often carrying the guitar he had saved up for. In addition his interest in buses had become almost fanatical. He seemed to know the timetables and routes of every Ribble bus service in Lancashire by heart, and began to travel on the buses on his own in the same way that train spotters spent their weekends on stations. He enjoyed travelling to new places as much as the rest of the family, but not physical exertion, so it suited him. He was equally dedicated to the ATC, which occupied a great deal of his time, and used to regale me with tales of what he did, make me envious of his flying practice in the Link Trainer, and bring me biscuits home. Never one to miss an opportunity, finding that his fellow cadets hankered after biscuits at their break-time, he arranged to buy Wagon Wheels in bulk from a grocer on Victoria Street which he then sold to them at a profit – slightly reduced by always saving one for me. It was some compensation for the loss of the surprisingly well-chosen presents he had always brought back for me from his Scout camps, of which the best was a jet pendant from Whitby. David being male, my father imposed few restrictions on his going out, but even so I was sure he was not always where he said he was. Though I teased him about it, I never disclosed the existence of the string ties he had hidden in the bedroom and took with him at night to change into.

There was one joint outing, however, which shook both of us. We had always been fond of our Uncle Frank. Not only much younger than our father and less censorious, he was generally great fun and had a fund of stories with which he used to entertain us all, often derived from his work. Though he once told me that whatever I decided to do when I grew up I should not join the police force, he himself loved the job. Sometimes David and I walked the five or six miles to see him and Aunty Mary, whom I also adored, and play with our two young cousins.

Our route was over Billinge End Road, down through Alum Scar and finally through the fields between Salmesbury Bottoms and Stanley Grange, which was where we came to grief. There were often cattle in the fields but we, who had withstood the threat of the bull in Cornwall at the tender ages of five and eight and a half, and had seen cows dispersed by a raised stick or clapped hands on rambles for years, were completely unworried. But all that was to change, in my case for ever.

The cause of the problem was the dog. As he trotted across the field just ahead of us, one after another the cows turned to look at him, some beginning to moo. Then, as we watched, one began to move towards him, and others followed. I began to be concerned for the dog but David assured me he could outrun them. Peter's tail went down between his legs, he paused, looked at the cows and then did run – back to us. Now the whole herd was coming our way and though David, now 15 or 16 and quite big, waved his arms, clapped and shouted, they just kept coming as we walked faster and faster.

'See that gap in the hedge,' he muttered, 'the bit with just wire? It's closer than the stile. Head for that, but don't run.' As we changed direction, the dog still with us, the leading cow let out a fearsome bellow and broke into a trot. Within seconds the whole herd was pounding towards us. As I fled after David, the dog streaking ahead, I could hear hooves drumming behind me, louder and louder. Utterly terrified I ran like a wild thing, heart beating madly, gasping for breath, sure that I was done for. In a final desperate effort, with snorts and bellows filling my ears, I dived head first under the barbed wire that David was holding up, and lay in an exhausted heap. When I gathered my wits I saw that the cows were now standing quietly on their side of the fence, still staring at the dog, but with no sign of aggression. It was as if the whole incident had never taken place.

Holiday Halts

At some time my mother's family had developed a tradition of an annual holiday in Silverdale which had been extended to include friends, spouses, in-laws and grandchildren, and was eventually to become a regular, shared Whitsuntide holiday for us, that is the two surviving sisters together with their husbands and children. Silverdale was soon dropped in favour of Grange-over-Sands, which became as familiar to me as Blackburn. We all lodged in the same house at first, with a Mrs Vickers in Grange Fell Road, but then separated, so that by the time I went to the High School we were regular fixtures with Mrs Fowler, on Fernleigh Road, where we remained until my last visit in 1958, most of which I spent revising for my A level exams. The bedroom I shared with my parents provided a spectacular view across Morecambe Bay to Arnside and Silverdale. When I was young, sent to bed before dark, I used to kneel at the window watching the play of light on sand and sea, drifting towards sleep with the shifting tide, the words of Guide taps in my head, '*Day is done, gone the sun, from the sea, from the hills, from the sky...*'

Our accommodation there was bed, breakfast and evening meal, the food prepared by Mrs Fowler but provided by my mother, a system which meant that most mornings saw me going with her to the grocer's by the fire station before the day's activities could really begin. Though these holidays still included walking, when I was small they were primarily seaside holidays, with more time devoted to playing on the beach or feeding the ducks in the Ornamental Gardens. Often, then, our walks were wet weather amusements, since Grange did not offer much indoor entertainment beyond money-hungry shops and cafés, but a different pattern had established itself by the time I reached secondary school age.

On most days our family went walking, sometimes taking Christine with us but never her parents, who were not walkers. The walks varied but always included Hampsfell and its Hospice, and with them Cartmel, together with a train ride across the viaduct for a circuit of Silverdale's cliffs and coves, past Arnside Tower and back over Arnside Knott. Years later my father claimed that he tied one of the pairs of knotted saplings which stood near the top, and I have no reason to disbelieve him. At other times our two sets of parents went off together for an hour or so, sometimes in Uncle Billy's car, leaving me, Christine and David to amuse ourselves in the open-air swimming pool, on the seafront or in the parks, shops and streets.

Having saved up for our holidays we could afford to buy ice creams, waste pennies stamping our names on strips of metal at the machine which stood on the Esplanade against the station wall, and buy trinkets, or in David's case, food. Christine and I frequented a shop in the main street to watch small items on sale such as rubbers and rulers being decorated by hand, though all I can remember buying there is a penknife. She bought one too, but had to hide hers for fear Aunty Jessie would confiscate it. I had no such problems. The two-inch knife, its blade bright to this day though with its pearl handle sadly chipped, became my pencil sharpener and was in my satchel on my first day at Crosshill – where I also used it to carve my initials on my desk lid. Sometimes David left us in Grange and wandered off on his own, and on one occasion was so late back for tea that my parents became quite anxious. They accepted his excuse of not realising what time it was and gave us both watches the following Christmas, but I knew that was not the whole story. He had walked across the railway viaduct to Arnside and been held up waiting to cross back between trains.

My walks were much more prosaic, through the trim public gardens or along the Esplanade, which I thought a lovely place. It was beautifully kept, with massed shrubs and fragrant flowers fronted by purple aubretia cascading over low limestone walls on one side. Since we were always there in spring, bees hummed in the golden senecio and birds fluttered and chirped in the branches. When the tide was in, waves washed against the sea wall on the other side. In some stretches dark-green turf, cut by water channels and broken by patches of sea pinks, fringed the foot of the wall, in others it was exposed rock and pebbles and, elsewhere, long stretches of sand which culminated in the bathing beach close to Holme Island. With the tide out, the three of us had a glorious time jumping the inlets, stamping the sand into jelly, damming the rivulets and destroying the stone towers we built. We also regularly made a circuit of Holme Island itself, not easily done by even we practised intruders on private property. The tide had to be right, and it was a quite a walk to get there, along the road and past the camping coaches in the railway siding that I always wished we could spend our holiday in. They seemed so much more romantic than houses.

At the other end of the Esplanade we spent many hours in the open-air swimming pool or sunning ourselves on its surrounding concrete tiers, both on our own and with our parents, but though I thoroughly enjoyed splashing about, no one could coax me out of my depth so I could only watch enviously as others hurtled down the water chute. My parents' favourite lounging spot, however, was outside the baths, on the beach to the south of it where the structure provided a seat for my mother and a stretching out space for my sun-loving father, as well as areas of rock, shingle and sand for me and David. It was essential to get there early, though, as space was limited to a handful of people. There was a handy café behind the baths, pitch-and-putt just inland at Berners Close and public tennis courts nearby, together with a bowling green where my father taught me to play.

Grange was a lovely place to be – until it rained. Then, apart from the treat of a visit to the Hazelmere Café, where my brother always had to be restrained from grabbing the biggest and best cake from the tiered stand when it was not his turn to choose first, it was not. There was little to do but read, which was fine, but the reading frequently took place in cold shelters, notably one in the Ornamental Gardens, well away from the windy seafront, to the accompaniment of raindrops drumming on the wooden roof and splashing about our feet. It was bliss when teatime arrived and we could go back inside our boarding house.

Once we were inside in the evening we tended to stay there, playing games, listening to the wireless or again reading, though when it was not raining we normally went down to the railway at 9pm to watch the mail train, a much-loved part of the holiday for me. As the bright red coaches thundered by, not only was it possible to see the postal workers inside sorting mail into pigeonholes, but also to watch a mechanism on the side of the train grab the bag of Grange's mail, suspended from a gantry at the side of the track, and swing it aboard. It thrilled me as much the last time I saw it as it did the first, when I eagerly entered it in my copy of *I-Spy on a Train Journey*.

David and I were both devotees of *I-Spy* books, the roughly A6-sized notebooks covering practically everything visible in the world about us in which children could record what they had seen. Though they were issued by the *News Chronicle*, being a member of the I-Spy Tribe and purchasing the books was not dependent on buying the paper, though it did contain a regular column written by Big Chief I-Spy, which we looked at occasionally in the library. I had several of the 40 or so books available, including birds, dogs, churches and buildings – for which I never did find a cruck cottage – and took them everywhere. For me journeys were never boring, just opportunities to add more sightings to my books.

The trains volume was particularly useful in keeping both me and David amused on our other regular holiday in Wakes Week. Once my father was settled in his teaching job our summer holiday week became more flexible, but until then we took our holiday at the same time as everyone else, though we stayed at home to do it. Thus we suffered the inconvenience of living in what was effectively a closed town. It was easier when the one week was extended to two and some shops did open in one of them, but initially we had to go a long way if we needed to buy anything but the morning paper. Jackson's, the newspaper shop on Revidge, opened briefly in the morning for people to collect their papers, but there was no delivery, something I made money out of. I collected not only my father's paper but also those for anyone else in Whinfield Place who wanted one, and to my surprise they paid me. Indeed, the two ladies who seemed to inhabit the kitchen of Beardwood Bank, across the lane, also supplied me with tea and biscuits.

Instead of going to stay in Blackpool, Morecambe or Southport, as a large proportion of the townspeople did, we had seven-day railway runabout tickets which took us to the seaside, but also to the Dales, the Lake District and North Wales. I enjoyed both the travel and the variety; perhaps one day playing on the beach in Morecambe and the next scrambling along Striding Edge, although not all our outings were trouble free. A trip we made to Liverpool to ride on the overhead railway along the docks was not entirely successful. I enjoyed the ride but was put off the city by poor weather and a vast crowd of workmen holding a rowdy meeting at Pierhead which rather alarmed me.

Another excursion was almost a complete disaster. We were off to Blackpool, so joined one of the many carefully controlled queues which stretched all the way down the station approach, round the booking hall and out onto the Boulevard. It was a bright morning with the prospect of a warm day on the beach, sea bathing, donkey rides and perhaps a visit to the Pleasure Beach, delights far removed from the quiet joys of Grange. In pursuit of all this I endured the long wait, the stuffy carriage in the overcrowded train and David's teasing with a minimum of complaint. One of the advantages of the runabout tickets was being able to take the dog with us, or even leave him at home on shorter days, so I was also hanging on to him until we finally reached Blackpool and I could release him to follow us.

Despite our having risen early and travelled on a direct excursion train, it was late morning when we arrived, so my father decided we would buy an early lunch which would enable us to spend the rest of the day uninterrupted. Then began a ritual which I hated so much that even now I quail at the thought of having to find somewhere to eat in a strange town, and find myself entering the first establishment I see. We walked through the centre, traversing street after street, my mother glancing longingly at interesting shop windows and both our parents eyeing up cafés, menus and prices. Meanwhile, my brother and I grew increasingly bored and cross.

'This one looks all right,' David offered from time to time.

'My feet hurt. Can't we just go in here?' I moaned, but all to no avail. My father was a meat and two vegetables man, very fussy about his food, averse to such common ingredients as carrots and tomatoes and above all, allergic to onions. On the rare occasions we ate out that almost invariably resulted in fish and chips. Even when we began to visit Manchester, if we wanted more than a snack in the Kardomah Café, it was the UCP for steak pudding and chips. The lengthy searches in strange towns were because my mother would have liked something different, but she was rarely successful, and once more it came down to a choice of chip shops. At last we went into one, by which time we were a very irritated father, an upset mother and two sullen children who could see their day on the beach rapidly disappearing. It was not a happy meal, but quickly over, and at last we headed for the shore.

Once there my father hired a couple of deck chairs and, as we began to change into bathing costumes, my mother settled into one of them, only to sit up suddenly exclaiming, 'Where's the dog?' We looked around us. There was no dog to be seen.

'You had him,' David started, looking at me.

'Stop that,' my father interrupted. 'I can't remember when I last saw him. Can you?' No one could, so there was nothing to do but go and search for him. It was awful. Back to the station we went and tried to retrace our steps through the now crowded streets, looking everywhere, wandering down side alleys, calling, whistling and asking people, but finding no dog. It seemed hopeless, and I became more and more miserable as we walked further and further. I could see no chance of finding one small black dog in the whole of Blackpool, but was in anguish at the thought of having to go home and leave him there. We got closer and closer to the chip shop, the short road to the beach and the end of our circuit. Still no Peter. Despondently, I trudged round the last corner. 'He's there! He's there!' I yelled as I sped along the street to fling my arms around him – and there indeed he was, sitting patiently outside the café door. We did manage a paddle, a Punch and Judy Show and donkey rides before we had to go for the train, but overall we might just as well have stayed at home.

The first train journey I made on my own was, in a very different way, even more of a disaster. I missed Ian, my old dancing partner, so when his mother invited me to visit them in their new home in Bournemouth and my parents agreed that I could go I was delighted, and I was quite prepared to accept their conditions. Thus I trailed behind my mother without protest as she walked along the Manchester platform, peering into the coaches to find me somewhere suitable to sit once she had let the guard know he had an unescorted little girl aboard. Eventually she was satisfied. 'This will do,' she muttered. 'In you get. You'll be all right in here.' I soon understood why. The coach had tables, not at all like the trains I was used to with compartments for six or eight, each with its own door or opening into a side corridor or the platform, and she led me to a table near the entrance where a pleasant-looking woman was sitting opposite a boy a little older than me. She smiled as we approached, and made to move her bag from the seat beside her to the rack.

'There's room here,' she offered. Mother smiled at her, as I lurked in the background.

'Thank you. I'm not actually travelling. But my daughter's going to be on her own, all the way to Bournemouth. I wonder, would you mind if she sat with you?'

'Of course not. She's very welcome, and I'll see she gets there all right. Why don't you sit next to William, dear, then you can talk to each other? What's your name?'

'Joan,' I said warily, though Mother seemed to have done quite well here. The woman seemed nice and I could always read my book if her son was hard to talk to. I glanced at him – jacket and tie, clean shirt, thin, with mousy hair and not too many spots, quite ordinary looking really. He seemed glum though. Perhaps he felt too old to be with his mother, or embarrassed by her remarks. I knew that feeling. My mother had put my case on the rack and was beginning to fidget in case the train set off while she was still on it. I was certainly not going to kiss her goodbye while he was staring, so instead of sitting down I said I would be back and followed her to the door.

'Behave yourself while you're there and don't forget your manners. Offer to do the washing up and whatnot. Oh, and remember me to Phyllis and ask her to let you phone when you arrive. And the postcard. Don't forget we'll be looking out for that.'

'Yes, Mother. OK.' This was going on too long. I just wanted to go now. I was relieved when I saw the train was ready to depart.

'Enjoy yourself, love. We'll miss you.' A quick hug through the window and I was off, waving until she was out of sight and all I could see was the end of the platform with the usual grey huddle of train spotters busy with their notebooks.

Rather pleased to be on my own, I stood by the door for a while watching the unfamiliar scenery. In the near distance grimy buildings broke the skyline, sooty smoke from mill chimneys drifting above them in the light wind, clouding the blue sky. Closer to me trains clanked and groaned as they shunted up and down the rows of rails in the goods yard. I could see men walking among them, some with metal bars, busy disconnecting wagons, one with a red flag walking between the rails in front of a train. Seeing them made me wonder if they ever got squashed. As I turned to watch, we abruptly rattled over points, moving rapidly from line to line. Briefly a train thundered by in the other direction, cutting off my view and drumming in my head. I caught glimpses of people looking out at me, a dining car with white cloths and table lamps glowing orange. Then it was gone, and the view different.

Now my eye was caught by soberly clad people clustered in dingy streets. I saw the backs of brick terraces, some neat and tidy, others with junk piled up in their tiny yards. In one a frenzied terrier barked silently at the train. Better houses came next, some with gardens, until at last there were open spaces, trees, fields and farms. It seemed to take hours to reach the edge of the city, far, far longer than leaving Blackburn, the end of which was signalled almost before anyone could settle down by the appearance of Darwen Tower. I wondered briefly what Bournemouth would be like, if it would be different from Manchester. I had seen postcards of beaches and cliffs and knew Ian thought it much better than Nelson, but other than that I knew nothing about it. Distracted from the view, I began to think more about my journey.

I was not sure that I wanted to sit next to glum-looking William for several hours, but knowing I had been left with no choice I eventually returned to the compartment to find him sprawled across both seats with a book in front of him, though he was actually glowering through the window.

'Move up, William. Let Joan sit down. That's better. Everything all right, dear? Your mother got off the train in time?' She laughed, so I smiled politely and she prattled on. She and William were going to visit her sister. She had not seen her for such a long time. William was so looking forward to it, wasn't he? His response was a unintelligible grunt.

'Have you been before?' I tried, turning to him.

'Yeah,' he replied, to the table.

'What's it like? Is it nice?'

'It's OK.' I gave up. He was certainly not going to be any fun. So much for my mother's choice. His mother, however, made up for his sullen silence, managing to ask me about myself and my doings as well as divulging her family history, and I found I enjoyed talking to her. When dinner time arrived she delved into her bag, ready to share their food with me until I produced my sandwiches, but after that she settled into a magazine, and I was free to read my book.

William was now reading as well, his eyes fixed on the page, but was once more encroaching on my space. I could feel his leg hot against mine, and did not like it. I wriggled a bit in the hope that he would realise what he was doing and tried to catch his eye, but his gaze remained on his book. Rather cross, I moved my leg away and went on reading. A short time later his leg was there again. Stupid idiot, I thought. Surely one seat was enough for him, unless – and suddenly I was hot all over and could feel my neck prickling with alarm at the very idea – unless he was doing this on purpose. Was this making advances? But this was a ridiculous idea. He had not even spoken to me directly, and his mother was sitting 3ft away, smiling at me over her magazine as I looked across at her. I gave myself a mental shake as I moved to the end of the seat. I must be imagining things. But within minutes that hot leg was there again, now moving gently against mine. Not only that, but from the corner of my eye I glimpsed William's hand slide from the table to rest on his knee, though still his head remained bent over his book.

I could feel panic rising. This had to be one of the unspecified perils my mother had been trying to protect me from, but she had failed. What on earth could I do? Perhaps I should tell the guard. After all, I was nominally in his charge. But he might not appear before that threatening hand shifted to my knee. My stomach went cold at the very idea. And would the guard even believe me? And anyway, what could I tell him? What words would I use; just say that William kept moving closer? How silly that would sound, complaining about nothing more than a boy wanting more space for his long legs, as I had at first thought. It was impossible. I was trapped, and he knew it. His eyes were still averted, but there was now a nasty smirk round his mouth.

I thought about shouting at him, simply telling him to stop, but that would be to admit that I knew what he was doing and bring his mother into it. Perhaps I should just tell her. But again, how? It all seemed so unreal, even to me. I looked across at her, now dozing over her magazine, so kind, so friendly, so normal. What would I say? Excuse me, your son's – your son's what? I didn't even have a name for what her son was up to. And again, William would just deny it, and where would that leave me? Looking very small and foolish. I could not do it. Escaping to the lavatory might help briefly, but I knew he would still be there when I got back and the whole thing would start again. Moving to another seat would be unacceptably rude to his mother and demand explanations I could not give. I was in despair. Huddled in the corner of the seat, my skin crawled as I felt William's knuckles begin to move against my knee. Instinct came to my rescue. Withdrawing as far as I could, I gave the offending leg a hefty kick.

Within seconds William was back in his own corner, staring out of the window, where he remained for the rest of the uncomfortable journey as my heartbeat gradually slowed to normal and I found peace in the pages of my book. Nevertheless, at the end of the journey when Ian's mother met me with a big hug, I burst into tears of relief. With Ian in attendance, and his father there to carry my case and drive us home I did not explain my reaction, but she got the story out of me later. By then it was little more than that a boy on the train kept rubbing up against me so I kicked him, but she contrived to make me feel much better about it. I assume she also told my mother as, although nothing was said about it when I got home, there were no more long, unaccompanied train journeys. Until I left home, I was only to see Ian and his family again when they came to stay with their relatives in Blackburn.

Pulling Away

As the rest of us busied ourselves with our own interests, my mother also started to extend her activities. As long as I had been at St Silas' she had been there when I got back from school, and I had felt the difference when I went to Caroline's house as I sometimes did before going home. I was met at the top of the lane and escorted to our back door by a prancing, tail-wagging dog, to chatter to my mother in the kitchen where she might be baking or cutting the bread for tea, or sit down with her for a drink by the fire while the cat purred around my feet. When I went to Caroline's house it seemed chill from its daytime emptiness, waiting for Caroline and her brothers to light the fire and have the tea ready by the time their father got home from work. Normally home first, she was responsible for the fire, which we sometimes lit between us, me usually rolling old newspapers to make firelighters while she chopped kindling. Naturally I wanted to do that too, so it is to Caroline that I owe my ability to wield an axe to split wood. That was my father's job in our house, and he would never have let me risk my fingers on it.

But the pattern was changing. Mother was still there to greet me on Mondays because it was wash day; fine on a good day when the washing could dry on the line, but dismal on a wet one, especially in winter. Then I arrived home to find the house smelling of damp washing and the only way I could get any warmth was to join the dog on the hearthrug inside the square the maiden formed with the fire. I used to wish we had a ceiling rack as Aunty Mary did, but Mother would never have had her washing hanging permanently in the living room. As soon as my father came home it was moved anyway, into the unheated front room to be brought out again on Tuesday.

On Tuesdays and Thursdays I now had to fetch the key from its hiding place and let myself in to await my mother's return from one or other of the cookery, craft and sewing classes she was increasingly attending, for pleasure as much as necessity by this time. I soon knew the names and histories of the women she met there, and of her teachers. She was particularly impressed by the lady who taught tailoring and dressmaking, who encouraged her to draft more of her own patterns rather than adhering to, or altering, the commercial paper patterns she had always used. One of her triumphs was a beautiful red coat she made for me, struggling for hours to get the sleeves to fit properly. For that, and later garments, I sometimes had to go into town after school for fittings at her classes. The ladies there were pleasant enough, but even at home I was impatient at being measured and pinned and made to stand on the table for a hem to be fixed, and doing so in public was even worse. Not only that, but on my first appearance comments such as 'Oh, hello. You must be Joan,' made me realise to my dismay that they knew as much about me as I knew about them. However, I appreciated my new clothes and what my mother made in the cookery classes, which she attended entirely for pleasure.

Mother had no need to go to cookery classes; she was a brilliant cook who, during rationing, held a reputation for achieving amazing things with dried egg and managed to work with my father's food fads and allergies to provide us with tasty meals. Not that I was aware of it at the time, other than in having to help remove the pieces of carrot from my father's portion of the broth we regularly dined on, and knowing that unless I ate what was put in front of me there would be no pudding. Our meals were, I suppose, fairly basic, with potatoes and other vegetables from my father's plot together with cheap cuts of meat or fish, but Mother also had her specialities, which I wish I could replicate.

One of these was mouth-watering potted meat made from shin beef, which I could smell as soon as I opened the back door on the days she made it. It drove the cat and dog as frantic as when she boiled up the butcher's scraps or fish heads for them, a smell which kept me out of the kitchen altogether. Another of her specials, and my father's favourite, was potato pie. That was so good that though she made a special onion-free one for us to take to the Ramblers' annual hot pot supper, there was always a queue waiting to finish up what we had not eaten. Part of the attraction was her pastry, deliciously light and crisp, which also contributed to my predilection for her steak and kidney pies and custard tarts, though all her pastry dishes and cakes were scrumptious. She had inherited some recipes from her mother, others she took from the Be-Ro or McDougalls flour company books, but her cookery bible was a much-thumbed and yellowing copy of *The Olio Cookery Book*, which I wish I had.

My mother continued to be there on Wednesdays when I reached home, but rarely alone. Mrs Ashton, one of her long-standing friends, who had at one time been among the evening visitors to our house, was normally there. Like me, her younger child, yet another David, had grown old enough to look after himself after school, freeing her to make weekly calls on my mother for gossip and the exchange of magazines.

Mother was neither a great reader nor terribly sympathetic to the rest of us who were. 'Take your nose out of that book and listen to me!' she used to insist, frustrated by the skill all three of us had in responding appropriately to what she said without taking in anything at all. She did, however, read magazines, treating herself to one a week, though not necessarily the same one, in much the same way that David and I had always been restricted to one comic each, which we had changed as we grew older. I had an advantage in that I could enjoy David's *Dandy*,

Beano and Eagle, while he was not attracted by *Girls' Chrystal, Schoolfriend* or *Bunty,* which were among my alternative choices. Our Christmas presents invariably included the appropriate annuals, one of which, a *Girls' Chrystal Annual,* I hid in my orange-box cupboard because one of the stories frightened me so much. I took it out periodically to read the other tales, but always put it back in its hiding place.

Mother's magazines were largely useful ones: *Woman, Woman's Own* and especially *Woman's Weekly,* which contained articles, recipes, knitting patterns and household hints, with a token story or two, but Mrs Ashton brought fiction in the form of *The People's Friend.* Thus I was able to add the surreptitious reading of romantic short stories to my regular diet of library books, school readers, adult thrillers such as Lesley Charteris's Saint books, which David was supposed to hide from me, and anything else I could find about the house. That principally amounted to *Lancashire Witches, Lorna Doone* and *The Forsyte Saga.* My mother was not happy when she saw me with the last one, but I heard my father say it would be fine because I would not understand the elements she was concerned about. He was right, even though I then looked for some.

Mrs Ashton was a lovely lady, though very different from my mother. I enjoyed joining them for tea when I got home. Since I was no longer a small child who was expected to be quiet, and my father was not there to inhibit me, I could converse, express my own opinions and listen to her views on and knowledge of a world I knew nothing about. She had relations in America, knew some film director personally, could talk about places she had seen in London and was an ardent royalist and avid reader of the articles written by Crawfie, the subsequently discredited royal nanny. Mrs Ashton was also a fan of Patience Strong, so I was introduced to her brand of poetry straight from Kenneth Grahame's dabbling ducks in my cherished Parnassus Poetry books long before school offered me anything different. She had a way of talking which gave a sense of drama to the most insignificant matters and greeted my appearance with such enthusiasm and interest in my affairs that I was always pleased to hear murmured conversation and find her hatted figure comfortably squeezed into my mother's chair when I arrived home.

Mother's magazines actually proved useful for me in my first Christmas at Crosshill. My sole charity effort at junior school had been to sell *Sunny Smiles,* pictures of smiling orphan babies provided in a little book rather like raffle tickets. Now I found that at Christmas I had to provide a home-made toy for a poor child, and *Woman's Weekly* proved a fertile source of inspiration. That first year I made a doll I would have been quite happy to keep for myself from an old sock and a few bits and pieces. I also went carol singing for the first time, to collect money for the local paper's Santa Claus fund.

It was the week before Christmas as we stood at Billinge End discussing the route, our breath curling in the cold air. 'Where first?' asked Betty.

'Revidge?'

'No, 'cos we're going to finish there, at Miss Lambert's.'

'What about Meins Road? They're big houses. Should be rich. Or is that too far?'

'Oh, come on!' Caroline moaned. 'I'm cold and we're never going to get anywhere. Let's start over there, do the streets round St Silas' and then up by the park to Revidge. OK? Who's got the tin?' Marjorie waved the empty collecting box and we passed through the nearby gates to a terrace of two or three big houses to stop at the first where lights were showing. A bit more time wasted deciding what to sing, and then we were ready.

'*Once…*'

'*Once…*'

We collapsed into stifled giggles, then tried again. This time I counted us in.

'*Once in royal David's city…*'

We need not have worried. Though we rang the bell twice no one came, so we moved to the next house where we tried again with rather less enthusiasm, but found a completely different reception. An elderly gentleman opened the door, listened to our explanation, said they had not been able to hear us properly and asked us to sing again. When we had done so he thanked us, said we would be welcome the following year and put the first of many donations into our tin.

Before long we found ourselves outside the home of one of our teachers, Miss Murphy. 'Should we?' Betty wondered, but the rest of us were already gathering by the door, ready to do our best. Tutored by Miggy at St Silas' and Miss Imisson at Crosshill, we could really sing. As our voices soared, clear and true, bearing the well-known words through the frosty air to the star-strewn sky, I found myself moved by our own music. During the evening we joked, chattered, were entertained to mince pies and pop by another of our teachers and enjoyed ourselves enormously as well as earning a fair amount of money. My clearest memory, however, is of those few moments on Miss Murphy's doorstep, when I sensed a spiritual universe.

Both carol singing and toy making continued for some time. In the following year, having had more warning, I knitted a kangaroo from yet another pattern in *Woman's Weekly*. Making things suited me, though sewing garments still held no appeal. Luckily we mostly did sample stitches in school, supported by instructions and extensive diagrams so that my drawing ability kept my marks high and provided me with a life-long reference book for sewing. However, the first task in my needlework lessons was to make a blue-and-white check apron and cap to wear in the domestic science lessons I would be having in the second year. I made a mess of it by cutting the pattern too small but it sufficed, particularly as I went into the arts form so only did one year of what we called cookery, though there was relatively little of that.

Domestic Science, the subject's official and more appropriate name, required two bus rides to Moss Street School since there was no provision for it on our premises, thereby occupying a whole morning. I chiefly remember the journeys for messing about on the top decks, making whistling noises with the paper bus tickets – for once not aided and abetted by Hilary, who was in the other half of the form – and being cluttered with satchel and basket. Once there, I was perfectly happy in the big, airy room, working away at its centrally placed wooden tables with a fire crackling merrily in the hearth at one end while Miss Hunt instructed me in the art of being 'The Ideal Homemaker', the topic for the first lesson. The requirements for this mythical person were cleanliness, thrift, capability, punctuality and neatness, as well as love and honesty, which were given prominence by being listed first and considered essential 'because the rest of the family will follow this example and so love and honesty will spread through the nation'.

Succeeding weeks were dedicated to dust, household cloths, shelves, the modern gas stove, cleaning metals, coping with fire, washing up and cleaning pans. Since we had to clean up the entire space before we left, taking it in turns to do one of the 14 tasks that involved, I also learnt the proper way to sweep a room and how to scrub a wooden table, a skill which I admit I still practise on the wooden boards I use in my own kitchen. Not until the end of the first term were we allowed to do any cooking. Then we made Christmas cakes, costed down to the last farthing at 2s 1¾d, excluding icing. Apart from jam slices, batter, blancmange, custard, scones and mock cream, the only other significant item was apple pie, which we made for our end-of-year exam. I had a moment of utter horror as we packed to leave when I discovered the sugar that should have been inside my rather splendid-looking pie still in my basket. On that occasion I managed to stifle my conscience and kept quiet.

We cooked no meals at all, but the final lessons included one on the value of vegetables and methods of cooking them to conserve food value and flavour, and another on food values in general and planning balanced meals. That involved food materials and groups, the latter being taught with the aid of some delightful verses. The one below covers the second of Miss Hunt's three food groups, which were body-building, protective and energy-giving.

Protective foods begin with V
Vitamins as in F and V   (Fruit & Vegetables)
Double M again and E and C   (Meat, Milk, Eggs & Cheese)
But also H, L, S and B   (Herring, Liver, Salmon & Butter)

These final lessons were really the only ones that dealt with anything I had not already learnt from my mother, but even so I was rather sorry when the sessions ended. I did not feel the same way about the needlework lessons, which I had to suffer for a further year.

I had other new lessons at secondary school of course, notably Mythology, Latin and French, the one serving to provide me with a knowledge of classical stories which proved invaluable in my later studies of literature, the other two demonstrating that I had little flair for languages other than my own. Latin became a problem to me in that I could never translate English into it with any facility, and though I eventually succeeded in French, I suffered from a lack of opportunity to speak it. I had a French pen friend, as we all did, with whom I corresponded laboriously throughout my school career, but with hardly enough room in our house for the four of us, I was unable to participate in the school's exchange programme.

The end of my two happy years at Crosshill coincided with a second royal event, the coronation of Queen Elizabeth II, though for me this celebration was tinged with sadness as a result of the unexpected death of my paternal grandfather a few weeks earlier. Still a Conservative councillor, and seeking re-election, he halted Clitheroe's municipal election by suffering a fatal heart attack during the night prior to it. In so doing he certainly made his mark: the situation was critical in that the gain of one seat would determine control of the council, it was too late to rearrange the election before the Coronation and, since he was Mayor Elect, the mayoral election also had to be rearranged.

Grandad had an impressive send-off, too. The funeral cortège, escorted by members of the Knights of St Columba as well as those of various other societies and youth groups he was associated with, and carrying a placard saying who he was, walked from his home to the Church of St Michael and St John in Lowergate led by the Mayor and other civic officials, but I was not there. As a child I was kept away from funerals and, as with so much in our home that really mattered, death and grief were not discussed openly. Our visits to Clitheroe declined after that, and they virtually ceased when Gladys remarried.

Though the Coronation was just as much a cause for national celebration as the Festival of Britain had been, and was marked by a wealth of activities at local level, it made far less impression on me than Blackburn's centenary had just two years earlier. I remember only that we were treated to orange squash at school, drunk from the Coronation mugs the town gave all its schoolchildren. The ceremony was discussed in lessons, however, and Mrs Ashton was full of it, so that I began to learn something of the British Monarchy and Constitution to add to my fading knowledge of the United States political system.

Aunty Jessie and Uncle Billy were among the thousands who bought their first television set in order to watch the ceremony. Thus the morning of the day that would also see the announcement of the first climbing of Everest by Sir Edmund Hillary and Sherpa Tensing, found us among the crowds of people flocking to the homes of friends and family to see the Coronation, many carrying Thermos flasks and bags of food. I was a great collector of scraps, until that time principally Gainsborough Ladies, which I long thought were a particular type of lady rather than portraits painted by Gainsborough, so had made a scrapbook using the specially produced Coronation scraps. Thus I had coloured pictures of the regalia, coaches and people involved, which was a great help as I watched the astonishing black and white pictures of the ceremony on television – the first time I had seen it. I was to learn that its arrival would bring a great change to our traditional family Christmas.

Christmas at our house began with setting our 18in high, artificial Christmas tree on the living room windowsill, decorating it with tinsel, topping it off with either a silver bell or a paper angel I had made in my origami phase, and finally putting candles in the holders on the ends of the branches. Even my feckless father only lit them once, to my mother's howls of protest, not surprising from someone who had been obliged to leave one house because of a fire. They were both less cautious with the nightlights inside the paper Chinese lanterns that we hung in both rooms, amid the festooned paper chains, some of which David and I made, though the crepe paper flowers were all my work. They lit the concertina-like lanterns for short periods when we were there to watch, but to my disappointment it was only the turnip heads we made at Halloween that were ever allowed to burn freely.

We always celebrated Christmas and New Year with Aunty Jessie, Uncle Billy and Christine, alternating the venues so that each sister only had to cook Christmas dinner every two years, and what I particularly liked about the preparations for their arrival was having both fires lit. In the middle of the afternoon my father built up the living room fire until it was a heap of glowing coals and then, as David and I watched from a safe distance and my mother stood by in case of accidents, he carried a shovelful into the front room. The scene is with me now.

The house is coldly bright from the wintry world outside, the shovel scrapes against the grate as my father bends to shuffle the red-hot coal onto it, and yellow tongues of flame lick back towards him as he walks, cautiously, from room to room. I feel the surge of heat as he passes me, breathe in the fumes and hear the satisfying swoosh as he empties his cargo of fire into the front room hearth. Soon the house will feel warm and I know that on this day it will remain so, even the bedrooms less chill with the rising air and warmth from both chimney breasts.

From where I stand I can see the Christmas cake I have helped to decorate positioned on the sideboard, next to the sherry bottle which has been extricated from the back of the larder where it spends the year. The pudding is steaming away on the stove and the chicken roasting in the oven, not quite masking the sweet smell of cooling mince pies. Everything seems to be waiting; shining clean and unusually tidy.

Once the visitors arrived, the pattern was always the same. David, Christine and I played with our Christmas presents, or squabbled over them, larked about outside if there was snow on the ground, or went for a walk with my father and Uncle Billy. Then came the meal, to be followed by games of some sort: jigsaws, snakes and ladders, ludo, draughts or cards, the card games becoming more sophisticated as we grew older. We moved from happy families to whist, then on to pontoon, which we played for matches. My father, always a keen card player and reputed to have done rather well from poker in his RAF days, always made up the foursome for the last one. For me those were evenings of sheer contentment, though I also enjoyed going to Aunty Jessie's, which brought some significant differences.

In the first place it began with a family walk over the tank, the common name for the entire hill on which the water tank stood, into the Howarths' more modern and so always slightly warmer house, and their front room with its superior Christmas tree. Of the few things for which I envied Christine, one was that Christmas tree. A much bigger version of ours, at about 3ft high, it stood on a low table to the right of the fireplace bearing not only baubles and tinsel, but also coloured lights – albeit plain ones wired up by a friend and painted by Uncle Billy. They were the cause of my envy. They captivated me, and throughout my childhood I yearned to have the same thing. I was also entranced by the different evening entertainment.

After tea Uncle Billy set up his cinematograph, a complicated-looking piece of machinery with wires and arms and wheels onto which he then proceeded to thread film, while I watched in great anticipation. That done, he set up a screen and, once the washing up and clearing up had been done and everybody settled in front of it, he turned out the lights and the show began. We laughed at the same films year after year: Charlie Chaplin, Laurel and Hardy and Mickey Mouse. I never tired of them. Those black-and-white images flickering across the screen, accompanied by the click and hum of the projector and occasional flarings from the fire, were my joyous introduction to the world of cinema. That was the element of our family Christmases that the advent of television eliminated.

What nothing could eliminate was the long walk home at the end of the evening. In the cold and dark, sometimes with snow or ice underfoot, stumbling back along the farm track and up the rutted path to the tank with no more than the feeble light of my father's torch to guide us, was far removed from the fun of running down it, crossing the back field and climbing the garden fence to avoid walking round. But the journey did have its compensations on clear or snowy nights. Then, once we reached Revidge, warm again from the climb, I could enjoy another annual treat. As we set out along Red Rake the whole town was spread beneath us, stars piercing the sky above, street lights twinkling through the darkness below. A child of the blackout, I was as enraptured by that view as when I eventually gazed over the lights of Hong Kong from the Peak.

When I was small, riding tiredly on my father's shoulders, I turned to watch until buildings obscured the lights. Then, enveloped in the sort of silence that only snow creates, broken by the crunch of its crust beneath our feet, our breath condensing in the cold air, we made our way down the hill, my parents exchanging greetings with other late revellers on the way. In later years, when David and I enlivened the journey with snowballing, kicking through snowdrifts and sliding along wheel ruts, that view still enchanted me, filling my sleepy head with the tracery of street lamps long after I could see it no more.

Off the Rails

Entering the third year at Blackburn Girls' High School meant moving to a more distant building on Preston New Road, just above the junction with Montague Street. Built in 1826 for Dr James Barlow, reputedly the first person in this country to perform a Caesarean operation, it was far more of a town house than a mansion, with none of the internal elegance of Crosshill. I was more taken with the rooms in the extension at the rear, particularly the hall on the first floor. Its polished parquet floor appealed to me as had the one at Crosshill, I was impressed by its organ and inspired by the honours boards hanging along one side recording the winners of major scholarships and awards. Just to see those was to want my name up there.

My form room was below the hall, at one end of the gym which we were not allowed to cross unless wearing gym shoes. Since the form room door was diagonally opposite the gym entrance, this was a regulation demanding to be flouted, but I was stopped in my tracks the first time I tried it. 'Joan Ryan, get off the gym floor and walk,' came a strident voice from behind me. What shook me was not the command, nor being caught, but the fact that a teacher entirely unknown to me knew exactly who I was, though I was now one among well over 300 girls.

Lessons that year had the occasional distraction of girls peering through the fanlight from the top of the climbing ropes, and were regularly accompanied by the muffled clatter of hanging bars being lowered, the clunk of balancing forms, vaulting horses and other equipment being moved about, the barking of instructions and crackly English or Scottish country dance music. In contrast, the gym was also the place where I first saw jive. It must have been a wet break or we would have been outside – or possibly hiding in the space beneath the organ – when two older girls put a record of their own onto the school gramophone and began to dance. Accustomed to sedate ballroom dancing, I watched in utter amazement as they stepped, twisted, turned and flung themselves and each other about with wonderful skill and precision. How I wished I could do the same. When they finally stopped I cheered as hard as anyone in the crowd that had formed around them.

Lack of space dictated that the gym was also the venue for medical inspections and injections, for which we lined up to be to be dealt with one at a time behind a small screen. We were still subject to visits from Nitty Norah the Bug Explorer, the nurse who came to look for lice in our hair, although few people had them at that age. I had caught them at St Silas', whereupon my mother had bought a dandruff comb to use in the treatment, which I dragged through my hair periodically for a long time afterwards. But the hair check was insignificant; what I really feared was the dental check. I no longer went to the school dentist for treatment, but my experiences there were such that an impending visit to any dentist brought a black cloud to my normally sunny existence, and to some extent still does.

The school dentist was located in the upper regions of a dismal office block at the junction of Richmond Terrace and Victoria Street. It was in itself dull, dingy and depressing, the bleak brown floors and dark green dados of its echoing corridors doing nothing to mitigate my sense of doom as I approached the waiting room, keeping very close to my equally silent mother. Once inside we joined the handful of people sitting around the walls. In that it was similar to a visit to the doctor, but there the resemblance ended. Since there was an appointment system the room was never quite as full, certainly with no one standing, but the chairs were hard and the people sitting on them all mothers and unhappy-looking children. Nor was there any space between the waiting room and the treatment room, so it was there that the first part of my ordeal began. Here I did not examine my surrounding or the people around me, or even stare at the floor. I could not shift my gaze from the half-glass door in the centre of one wall, which was all that stood between me and the dentist's chair. I imagined it there; back towards me, arms towards the window, enclosing its current victim.

As at the doctors I could see movements through frosted glass, but here I was also forced to listen to what was going on. My stomach sinking lower with every sound, I heard the moans and cries of the patient punctuating the sound of the drill, not the soothing hum of today's high-speed version, but something more akin to the throb of a workman's pneumatic machine. Would the dentist use it on me without anaesthetic, probing until I screamed; jab me with a needle so crude that it was, albeit more briefly, almost as painful; simply yank out a tooth or give me blissful gas first, so making me feel ill afterwards? I never knew what to expect, other than pain, and it was with sheer terror that I walked through the door from which my tearful predecessor had emerged, next on the conveyor belt. I do not know if my mother simply decided to take me elsewhere, or if I was refused further treatment, but this torture ended on the day I found the pain completely unbearable and bit the dentist.

The lack of space responsible for multi-use of the gym was prevalent in other aspects of school life. We had, for example, no playing fields. Fitted into the angle formed by the rear extension was a part sunken playground onto which the gym opened. It was the exact size of a netball court, so exact that throwing in a ball necessitated climbing up the surrounding rockery, which rather disconcerted and disadvantaged visiting teams. That, together with the small terrace which overlooked it, was the only outdoor space. For hockey, which now replaced rounders as our winter game, we had to walk the mile and a half to Blakey Moor Girls' School playing fields at Troy. That suited me, since it was virtually opposite our house, especially if the lesson was at the end of a morning or afternoon, or on Saturday mornings, when for a short period I had to turn up as a second team reserve, though I rarely played. Mostly I prepared refreshments in the nissen hut which served as our pavilion.

Sometimes my friends went home with me after hockey for a drink of pop, or on occasion, cider, to which my parents had a strange attitude. Though they were nominally teetotal, apart from a small glass of sherry for my father on Christmas Day, there was usually a bottle of cider in the kitchen. It stood alongside the soda siphon and bottles of lemonade or dandelion and burdock from which I normally drank, and I could have cider if I wanted. I knew it was alcoholic since it was not available at the grocers, and I sometimes accompanied my father to the side door of the Fox and Grapes at Limefield to buy it, presumably because the closer pubs on Revidge were not licensed for sales off the premises. However, the difference never registered, so I treated it as an alternative variety of pop. Since I was never expected to drink more than one glass of anything, it hardly mattered.

Just as we had no playing field on site for winter games, so we had no provision for summer ones. We walked to the top of Corporation Park to play tennis on the public courts there, and for athletics it was back to Troy. Addicted to the outdoors though I was, sport was never really my thing. I could reach the moderate pre-competition standard to earn the requisite points for my form for Sports Day, held at yet another venue, the East Lancashire Cricket Ground, but there was never any danger that my long-suffering mother would have to put in an appearance to watch me perform on the day. This was not true of Speech Day, which was regarded as a great event in the school year. I particularly remember 1953.

'Mum! Mum! Guess what!' I called as I rushed into the house, forgetting that Mrs Ashton would be there.

'What on earth's happened?' she replied, as they both turned to look at me.

'I've won a prize; for steady work at Crosshill. It's worth 10 shillings and I've got to go to Seed and Gabbut's next week and choose a book. And you and Dad get a special ticket to Speech Day, with seats in the balcony.'

'Goodness me!' said Mrs Ashton, before my mother could speak. 'Haven't you done well?' My mother gave me one of her sparkling smiles.

'Well done, love. You deserve it, and your father'll be really pleased. Has anyone else got one? Caroline? Hilary?'

'No, just me,' I answered gleefully, dancing around with delight before finally sitting down to join them.

The following week saw me in the bookshop with my mother, a note from school in my hand. Overwhelmed at first, I wandered from one set of shelves to another, wondering where to start. Since fiction was forbidden I headed to the art and craft section as I still did in the library, and tentatively took a book from the shelves. Unused to new books, or their brightly coloured covers, I felt uneasy handling them. Mother, my moral support, encouraged me by looking at some herself and making suggestions, most of which I dismissed irritably, but as I began to feel more comfortable, I started to enjoy browsing. I moved to history, geography, other subjects I was interested in, then back again. I knew I would only read those books once and wanted something more lasting. At last I had it: *Crafts for Recreation* by Evadna K. Perry which, the blurb told me, was 'the book for every woman who wants to do things with her hands.' I examined it closely, smelling its freshness, feeling the pristine pages. There were lots of ideas, clear instructions and illustrations. This was it. Then I looked at the price, 12s/6d. Gloom descended and I started to put it back, but Mother stopped me. 'Is that what you really want?' she asked. I nodded glumly. 'That's easy then. We'll pay the extra half crown. Come on.' I protested half-heartedly, then gratefully followed her to the counter where she explained and we left the book to be plated.

Before I saw it again I had been through both the intensive period of preparation which prefaced Speech Day each year, and most of the day itself: uniform inspection preceding the crocodile to the Cathedral; the silent wait in hard pews; the comfortingly familiar service, including the school's own arrangement of *God be in My Head*; Miss Armstrong's rendering of *Corinthians Bk.1, Ch.13* drifting in the vastness and, finally, the clear notes of the Dresden amen soaring aloft, presaging our release into a free afternoon. Newly washed, pressed and polished, I was now standing in King George's Hall, nervously waiting to collect the book.

I watched the poor girl who had been made to cross the platform three times in rehearsal, under instructions to improve her deportment, stump across the stage, shoulders bowed, head lowered, just as before. I glanced down at my deportment stripe and was reassured; thought about my first Speech Day, and was not. Having been selected in my first year to present the bouquet to the speaker – for no better reason than being the smallest child in the school – only a whispered, 'Not me, dear, the next lady,' had prevented my handing it to the wrong person. This time, again before a gathering of over a thousand, not only did I have to set off at the right time and avoid tripping on the steps and wires, but also remember to smile, take the book with my left hand and shake hands with the right at the same time as saying thank you and, worst of all, respond to anything the speaker might say. All I wanted now was for it to be over.

The queue shuffled forward as the names were read. I reached the bottom step, wiped my sticky palms on my gymslip ready for the handshake, and concentrated on the girl ahead of me. Oh no! The speaker was talking to her, prolonging my agony. At last she was on her way, passing the marker, the last chair. My turn.

Safely back in my seat, surreptitiously turning the pages of my prize during the subsequent speeches, I noticed a slip of paper inside it with the name and address of the donor, a Miss M. Towle of London, reminding me that I still had to produce a suitable thank-you letter. I did not then notice the publishers' notice from the first edition which begins 'Today (1944) anything suggestive of "fun" may appear at first sight misplaced' and goes on to defend recreation as a tonic for workers and the book as combining usefulness and pleasure.

I was soon back on the stage for an enthusiastic rendering of Handel's *March from Scipio* with the orchestra. Hidden away at the back of the second violins, one of many and not required to say anything, I relaxed, looked about me and tried to see my parents in the crowd. I was also confident that I could play the piece, which I fear was not the case later. As the years passed I made it to the front desk of the second violins, sitting next to Hilary who was the leader, but even in the sixth form there were a couple of bars in the *March from Carmen* that I could never guarantee to finger fast enough and usually pretended to play. At that stage the orchestra contained a very talented junior who could play better than any of us, and I tried hard not to hate her for it.

By the time I left school my violin reports, once good, had deteriorated to a simple 'poor'. As a competent sight reader I got away with a lot, but violin practice was never high on my list of priorities. Too often I turned up for my weekly incarceration in the far study with the long-suffering Mr Miller not having touched my violin since the previous lesson. I could blame this deficiency on the lack of somewhere to practise out of earshot of the rest of my family, or on the fact that Smoky, who had simply run away from my efforts on the recorder, began to howl continuously and try to claw her way up me to get at the source of the noise as soon as I drew the bow across the strings. These would, however, be pathetic excuses. There were just too many other things that I preferred to do.

The Speech Day entertainment included some dancing and lots of singing. The latter was a feature of the school, hardly surprising in an establishment which could boast Kathleen Ferrier as a former pupil, as indeed could St Silas', though she only attended there for a few months. Most of our music lessons I remember as being dedicated to singing and, though I had to memorise the notes since I never mastered reading music without my violin, I learnt enough to enjoy it thoroughly and never more so than at the end of Speech Day. The performances completed, the last words spoken (which in 1953 included a prayer for the new

Queen), the end of the evening in sight and the prospect of a holiday on the morrow, the assembled school rose to its feet as one, facing the darkened auditorium.

An anonymous figure in the rows of blue and white, I fixed my eyes on the conductor and waited. Miss Boyson broke the silence with a thunderous introduction on the organ, and the singing began. 'Oh Brother man fold to thy heart thy brother…' Ponderous stuff perhaps, but rousing, so that for me it was the thrill of *Merrie England* all over again, and this time I was wholly involved. The sheer volume of sound excited me, the feeling of being part of something so much greater than myself and, when the audience rose too, to lend its power to the three verses of the National Anthem, I thought it magnificent.

Not everything in my first year at the main school was so enjoyable. Life was becoming more complicated and the work harder. I found myself changing friends again, beginning to get into trouble, subject to a more rigorous discipline and responsible to a form teacher I did not get on with who was serving a less benign headmistress.

My worst trouble, in that it went beyond the classroom, stemmed from the Crush Club. In the first two years we juniors had seen little of the prefects, who seemed to us only slightly less awesome than the staff, but now they were before us all the time and objects of affection for some of my friends. While I admired one or two particular sixth formers from afar, perhaps blushed if they spoke to me and was anxious to please them, I was not truly afflicted by this adolescent passion for members of my own sex. Not for me any hanging about after school in the hope of seeing some senior girl, going out of my way to walk past her house or sending her a Valentine card. However, that rather left me out of things, which I did not like. My answer was to become the neutral chairman of the aforementioned club. As such, when someone was caught with a list of members, I was seen as the ringleader. That left me ashamed, embarrassed and uneasy about my position in school for many months – and able to recite Robert Browning's *Home Thoughts from Abroad* with hardly a pause for breath. My punishment was to learn the poem and recite it to the headmistress. Unfortunately I was so unnerved when I entered her office that I could remember nothing, so had to return on the Saturday morning to be tested by the school secretary.

As far as lessons were concerned, having achieved my prize for steady work, I slacked. As the customary 'good's on my work slipped to 'fairly good's I was accused of carelessness and lack of effort, but took no notice until, at the end of the year, my cosy little world was blown apart. My examination grades were generally mediocre, but only as Mrs Mercer read further and further through the Latin lists did I begin to worry. Eventually I heard my name – and 'fail'. In a state of shock I stared down at my desk as she went on talking, hearing nothing, my stomach an empty pit, tears pricking my eyes. It was the first time I had failed anything. Shame surged through me and also anger; with myself, my teacher, the school. And how could I face my parents? Knowing my report would soon drop through the letter box, and in any case too upset to keep my failure to myself, I trailed home miserably to confess. I was expecting ructions but it was their disappointment, not their anger, that made me vow to work harder.

Though I had further to go, I normally enjoyed my walk to the main school in its seasonal variations. On crisp autumn days I carelessly kicked apart the heaps of swept up leaves on the pavement, savouring the swish and crackle of the swirling colours, heedless of the hours of work that had gone into gathering them. Winter saw me rush through rain, cold and fog, and sometimes catch the bus, but summer was all pleasure. No more obligatory grey knee socks, gloved hands, blue striped scarf neatly tucked in, gabardine mac and hood covering the stiffened beret which had replaced my Crosshill bowler. Summer saw me dawdling home with friends, clad in white socks, navy blazer and blue-and-white daisy patterned dress. As only the material was regulation, mine were designed and made by my mother, so at least I had something individual.

We rarely went straight home but detoured via each other's houses, Enid, Hazel and I, at the end of the route, often lingering on Sacred Heart Church's low wall to collaborate over our homework before parting. Once off the main road, as long as we avoided our teachers' homes and kept a wary eye out for prefects, we dared to discard our hats and skim them across the road – playing Frisbee before the name was invented – and eat in the street. From time to time I treated myself to a peppermint choc ice from Brenton's on the corner of Granville Road, the only shop I knew that sold such things, but buying ice cream could be hazardous. Hilary, going home on the bus one day eating a cornet, was horrified to see the head girl climb on. Thrusting the ice cream into her pocket, she sat there helplessly as it melted, trickled through her clothes and ran down her leg, leaving her with an uncomfortable, sticky mess and her mother's eventual wrath.

Realising that I was encountering the same people every morning as they waited at bus stops or walked towards me, I entertained myself for a while on my way to school by eliciting greetings from all of them, as well as learning the registration numbers of the cars which regularly passed me. David usually passed me, too, travelling by bus as he had much further to go. He was still at the Technical High School, but soon destined to go to Cranwell and become a pilot – or so we thought. It was a disappointing shock when he turned out to be colour blind and so failed the final medical. Never a keen student, though he had worked hard to gain a place at Cranwell, he abandoned his A level examinations, left school and went to work in the Electricity Board offices in Jubilee Street while he waited for his National Service call-up papers.

I, busy with my own affairs, still very much a child and not much interested in what my almost adult brother was up to, saw less and less of him. He was out almost every night and I was aware that he was idling in coffee bars, listening to music, playing his guitar and spending some of his leisure time as a hospital DJ, but the outside world was his, not mine. Though my father was no Luddite – we had a telephone by 1947 – he considered television a potential distraction from studying and refused to have one until I left school, and the transistor radios that were appearing were beyond the reach of my savings. As a result of that, and my lack of inclination to argue with my father over his strict limits on my leisure activities, the burgeoning music scene and emerging teen culture virtually passed me by, even though Lionel Walmsley, one of my classmates at St Silas', was to become Lionel Morton of *The Four Pennies*.

Unscheduled Routes

As David stayed in Blackburn to pursue his own interests, and later to work, our holiday format changed. I found myself accompanying my parents to boarding houses in seaside resorts where walks in new areas could be combined with sightseeing or sunbathing, but often felt lonely without my brother. I saw other bored-looking youngsters my age with their parents and longed to talk to them, but never quite knew how to go about it. The one time I did have company was disastrous.

Within 18 months of leaving school David was in the RAF as he had always wanted to be, though as a technician, not a pilot. In the summer of 1955 he was stationed near Minehead, so that was where we went for our holidays. I had no quarrel with that; it was a new place and I wanted to see him. Furthermore it turned out that there were two children living in the house where we boarded, the elder one, Gill, slightly younger than me. We got on well together and she joined many of our outings, particularly to the beach, but so, unfortunately, did her younger sister Jennifer. She was my problem. Everything seemed fine and my parents were pleased for me to have company, but within days I was doing all I could to avoid her, without feeling able to explain why.

It started when the three of us were getting changed to go swimming. I had begun to develop a figure and was self conscious about it. Jennifer was about to make things worse. She came over and stood in front of me. 'You've got fat pimples,' she pronounced. 'Why've you got fat pimples?' I said nothing, but could feel my face reddening. Recognising my discomfiture, she pressed home her advantage. 'You've got fat pimples,' she chanted. 'You've got fat pimples.'

'Jennifer, be quiet! That's rude,' said her sister, but the damage was done. She said nothing more then, but for the rest of our stay, if no one else was in earshot, she sidled up and repeated her words. I enjoyed Gill's company, liked the area and appreciated the things we did, but not when Jennifer was about. Her tormenting reduced me to a state of confused misery, which I came to associate with Minehead, so have never felt inclined to visit it again. Nevertheless, I was glad we had gone to see David. Before long he was posted to Hong Kong so that our only contact for two years was via infrequent letters, one of them to report that the dog had been put down to end his old-age suffering.

Though David's bed remained in position ready for his coming home on leave, once he joined the RAF I effectively had a room to myself, but I was not satisfied. For years I had pestered my parents to let me use the screened-off storage space on the landing as a bedroom. Now my scheme was to put David's bed there so that he could have a place of his own for his short visits, while I would have room for a table and chair and somewhere to entertain my friends. I got the table, but that was all. It had to share the already cramped space with everything else.

I had wanted a table ever since the radiator had been fitted in the bedroom, so that I could do my homework there in peace. Thoroughly shaken by my third-year exam results I had applied myself more seriously to my studies so when the time came, my results generally being much the same level in all subjects apart from Latin, I found the choice between arts and science difficult. As with my selection of St Silas' Guides, my parents discussed the matter with me but made the decision mine. I finally opted for the arts and my only regret is that I was unable to study both history and geography. I have always felt my lack of historical knowledge – though never enough to drive me to do much about it. Having chosen my subjects, my ambition simply became to do well in the requisite eight 'O' levels while retaining some of my social activities.

Apart from Guides and the Rambling Club, I was largely restricted to church or school events, or occasionally a trip to the pictures with girls or boys my parents knew. I did not dare return from the cinema any later than the appointed time so it was always straight home, but since I did not yet hanker for what I saw as the high life – the Saturday night dances in King George's Hall – I did not much mind the restrictions. I was still content with what I had been involved in for years, and in spending time with my friends during the day.

I did sometimes go out in the evenings with my mother, though not always willingly. 'Why don't you go with her yourself?' I demanded angrily one day as my father once again suggested that I accompanied my mother to a film she wanted to see. 'Why do I always have to go? It should be you. I've got work to do as well!' I slammed out of the room, but in minutes I was back, apologising and ready to go, not because of the disagreement with my father, but because I could not bear to leave my mother upset for long.

As well as taking me to the cinema, Mother also occasionally took me to events in town in which my father had no interest, including a memorable violin act at the Palace Theatre on the Boulevard, a place which we normally only visited for pantomimes or shows by Blackburn Amateurs. As ever, I wriggled about in my red plush seat, waiting impatiently for something to happen, looking around for people I knew and studying the elaborate light fittings and trumpet blowing cherubs which ornamented the front of the balconies. When the lights dimmed I settled into the quiet, expecting the strains of violin music, but it was so much more than that. The violinist was a showman. He played everything from classical music to Irish jigs, but above all he played with the violin all over the place: above his head, behind his back and even with the bow through his legs. I sat and marvelled until it was time to join in with the final clapping and cheering. I enjoyed it immensely and went home determined to practise harder. Sadly, my resolution was short lived.

I was similarly inspired, though to better effect, by the ballet performances that Mother and I had begun to attend in Manchester, on trips organised by Miss Boderke. Though my ambition to be a ballerina had waned, my enthusiasm for dancing had not, so these trips were a tremendous treat, offering hours of enchantment completed by queuing for my programme to be autographed by the stars. Beryl Grey, I think, was one of them. Proficient in ballroom dancing, and with Ian no longer available as a partner, it was ballet and tap that held my interest and saw me performing in displays and music and drama festivals in Blackburn and elsewhere. Having completed all but the last ballet exam which would have qualified me to teach, I was in fact paying for my tap lessons by helping to teach younger ballet students.

My world was changing, but the Rambling Club still figured largely in it, both socially and in the rambles, which had begun to take place further afield. By the time Wainright published the first volume of his *Pictorial Guide to the Lakeland Fells* in 1955, I must already have climbed most of them. My father, who rarely took exception to anyone, had an unexplained dislike of Wainright, whom he knew, so I saw nothing of his books until I was much older. In any case I had no need to worry about where I was; I simply went where I was taken. Thus it is walks which had extra significance which rise as a faded patchwork from the recesses of my memory.

My clearest recollection of the Yorkshire Dales is not of a whole walk but of an incident during it. As I jumped happily from clint to clint across the limestone pavement at the top of Malham Cove, I was startled by an anguished scream. Turning, I saw that the same Elsie who had threatened to sink the boat when beating the bounds had fallen, and had one leg jammed in a grike. 'It's broken. I heard it crack,' someone stated. I gulped, feeling scared and slightly sick, and kept my distance as the club members gathered round, her husband bending over her moaning figure, talking reassuringly. She was quickly covered with coats and remained where she lay, white faced and unusually quiet, as one of the younger members raced away down the steep path towards Malham to fetch help. Meanwhile, the others stood around, discussing what to do. Remaining where I was I watched as some of the men, including my father, struggled to lift Elsie to the safer, grassy area before starting to carry her across the cropped, green turf towards the road, where another member had already gone in the hope of flagging down a car. As I sought out my mother and started to descend the rough path which ran by the side of the cove, I realised that my legs were trembling.

A pleasanter memory is of a day in the Lakes when Alan and I, always rambling companions, hurtled round the Fairfield Horseshoe behind our fathers at a speed dictated by the danger of missing the bus home. My mother had needed persuading to let me go, she and Alan's mother electing to walk at a lower level rather than rush, but I loved it. The weather was glorious, bright and clear, with views to the edge of a cloud-patterned landscape of shifting colour and changing light, though we had only a snatched sandwich break in which to absorb them as we sped along. I was elated by the sense of speed and urgency, running along the ridge for the sheer joy of it where the going was easy. There were just the four of us, and Peter of course, trotting effortlessly ahead or moving backwards and forwards, checking we were all there. Alan, my age but always faster and stronger, led the final descent on the steep path from end of the ridge, dark hair flopping over his face as usual, feet which seemed too big for his lanky frame threatening to make him trip, though he never did. 'Easy, Alan,' his father called. 'There's no rush now.'

Hearing that, as I scrambled down behind him, no longer invigorated by the euphoria that being on a mountain top still gives me, I felt my energy evaporate. It seemed a long way down, but I retained a tremendous sense of achievement, bolstered by my father who slowed to walk with me as I faltered.

I also recall taking Alan up Arnside Tower. It was early autumn and we were spending the weekend with the Ramblers at Arnside Youth Hostel, the original one on the hill behind the promenade shops. He was there with his parents and I enjoyed showing him all the features I knew so well from my holidays in Grange. Together we listened for the warning signal and watched the tidal bore, climbed up the angled blocks of stone to reach the end of the pier rather than walk out along it, and built and demolished pebble towers just as I always had with my brother. Saturday found us amid a cheerful group, still talking and laughing about the previous evening's film show.

The first problem had been finding the venue, the Village Hall or possibly the Women's Institute, but somewhere obscurely placed in the higgledy-piggledy streets at the top of the town. Lights were few and dim, so our party giggled and guffawed its way through the back alleys by torch light, causing a commotion by arriving just as the film was about to start. I forget the title but it reminded me of Uncle Billy's Christmas shows; the same black-and-white images, the same clicking reels and the same pauses to change them, but with a less inhibited audience. It was entertainingly riotous, and after it came another hilarious journey. 'This way,' someone called confidently, leading us into a cul-de-sac.

'No! No! It's along here.'

'Shhh, we're waking the whole of Arnside.'

We had just traversed the same route in daylight – and found it ridiculously simple – before starting the climb to Arnside Knot. Up ahead I could see the stile in the wall beside the solitary trees we were aiming for, and beyond it the wooded top of the hill. I disliked the rough field, so while Alan strode up it I went more slowly and turned at the top to take in the view. Sea and sand shimmered in sunlight; a train rumbled across the viaduct, the smoke from its funnel drifting in the still air as it headed towards Grange; Hampsfell rose beyond the town, its bare top leading my gaze to the right where the distant Lake District peaks serrated the horizon. Seagulls circled above my head as I gazed, their raucous calls a distraction from the twittering birdsong close by.

Beyond the stile the sandy path led across the hilltop and down past the knotted trees to the cool, forest track which met the road. As we emerged from the shade I could see the tower, but as we took the track towards it I moved to the middle of the party. The farm we were approaching not only had the filthiest and smelliest farmyard I knew, but also several dogs which barked ferociously with a furious rattling of chains as they leaped at us, restrained only by their collars and the kennels to which they were secured. Though Alan mocked, I kept well out of reach as we tramped through the mire which surrounded the abandoned vehicles and machinery fringing the yard. I negotiated the gate as quickly as possible, only to be met by a morass of mud and cow pat churned up by cows waiting to get into the yard to be milked. It sucked at my boots, threatening to cover them, and sending the smell with me. Beyond the sludge, we climbed a short distance into the field and stopped.

This was what I had been waiting for. 'Come on, Alan,' I urged. We should have time to climb it,' and as the adults settled and uncorked their flasks, he and I headed for the tower. As we did so I could hear my father, who was leading the walk, airing his local knowledge.

'It's a pele tower,' he was saying, 'built in the 14th or early 15th century as a refuge when people were under attack,' but I was soon out of earshot, clambering quickly over the crumbling limestone walls. The inside was a grassy square, open to the sky and empty but for sheep droppings and fallen stones.

'Which way?' Alan asked.

'Up there.' I pointed to where the remains of a staircase led upwards, its inner wall gone in places, the steps uneven, some broken, and he set off ahead of me. Untouched by the sun, the inside wall felt cold and clammy, but I forgot this as I scrambled onto the top to stand beside him, feeling the breeze lift my hair as I turned to look towards the estuary. We waved to our parents, saw that they were preparing to go and scrambled down to follow them, towards Silverdale, the seashore, and another of my favourite features of the walk.

I loved the mile or so of sand and sea turf fronting the shore, the dark green carpet criss-crossed with channels and pools. The adults kept close to the coast but Alan and I went far out, jumping the muddy channels, or pausing to see what the water held, before veering inland to visit a shallow cave. Finally we climbed up to the wooded cliff path which took us via sand and rock to the concrete walkway leading into Arnside. I was tired but content. 'It's been lovely today,' I whispered sleepily to my mother that night, as I snuggled into my bunk in the dormitory.

I was less happy with some of the local walks, particularly those dedicated to the collection of holly, whinberries and blackberries, though one year Peter enlivened the blackberry picking by rolling in the remains of something dead on the riverbank near Dinkley. He stank abominably, and the bottle of cheap scent I poured over him did not help at all. Picking holly I thought a pointless, prickly pastime as berried branches were available in Whinfield Place. As for the other two, I applied myself only because I knew I had to suffer the scratches if I wanted to enjoy Mother's blackberry jam and luscious pies – and I did. Sometimes she mixed the blackberries with apple, but the whinberries she always used on their own, both of them a delicious change in our diet for the short period they were available.

An advantage of the local walks was that Christine often came too, but by the mid-1950s she had largely abandoned the Rambling Club, and me, in favour of Cracker, the horse which she had saved up to buy. She had been riding other people's animals to victory in gymkhanas for years and was so keen to own one that until her parents eventually managed to persuade the school to let her cycle, she ran the mile and a half journey both ways every day to save her bus fare. I sometimes accompanied her to the smithy in Canterbury Street because I enjoyed the bustle of the place, the smoky red of the fire in the dim shed, the clang of metal on metal and the searing smell and hiss as the red-hot shoes were fitted. I also read pony books as avidly as anyone else, but I was no horse lover. Christine persuaded me to mount hers once, but made it trot along West Leigh Road rather than walk as she had promised. Thoroughly upset, thereafter I merely patted it tentatively or kept clear when she rode round to visit us. Hilary was more receptive, cantering off down the central reservation of the Arterial Road when offered a ride, but we both knew the animal had a mind of its own. She once ran to their front door in response to her mother's desperate shouts to find the horse standing in their hall. It had walked in when she opened the door to Christine, and it required the united efforts of all three of them to get it out.

My reason for gradually becoming less keen to go out with the Ramblers every Sunday and making schoolwork an excuse to stay at home was very different, but I was reluctant to admit to it. I wanted to go to church but not, I have to confess, because I had been overcome by religious fervour, but because the evening service on Sunday was the meeting place for the younger element of the parish, specifically in the back rows on the left-hand side. The hymn *Abide with Me,* which prefaced the end of the service and our release into conversation outside, conjures up visions of that shadowy, echoing corner, the hardness of the wooden pews, the smooth sandstone of the massive pillars and the warm sense of communal friendship. I felt I was missing out when I was not there, even though I had become less of a child and more a junior member of the Rambling Club, with friends there closer to my age.

That change enhanced both walks and social gatherings, particularly the games and dancing, where I was no longer a little girl among adults. I could participate on even terms and, while I mostly still shuffled round the dance floor with Alan, I now had other partners. Even so, I much preferred my very first one, my father. He was a superb dancer with a flair and panache which made being swept round the floor by him in a tango or quickstep a wonderful experience. I needed no *Strictly Come Dancing* show to reveal the true delights of the ballroom. My mother danced well, too, but there was no one in the club to touch him, and he had none of her dislike of the limelight. Quite the opposite in fact.

My father had remained active in footpath preservation, frequently checking paths on behalf of the national Rambling Association and going out on Sundays equipped with pliers and secateurs to deal with blocked stiles. In addition my parents now numbered the Council for the Preservation of Rural England among their activities where, as with the Liberal Party and anything else in which he was involved, my father was always ready to speak. My mother, on the other hand, only spoke in public once a year – and hated it.

The occasion was the Rambling Club AGM, where she had to speak in her capacity as Auditor. Her nerves began when the books appeared for audit, not because she had any difficulty with the figures, which kept her happily occupied for several evenings, but because she feared she might find a problem which would need comment. She never did, but just as I had been anxious about standing up alone on Speech Day, so she worried about standing up before an expectant audience of ramblers. Although able to laugh about it, she could not overcome her nervousness, and the teasing she received from the rest of us could not have helped. David, himself as able and entertaining a talker as both my father and Uncle Frank when he chose, was the worst offender, but we were all guilty. When the time arrived Mother sat miserably through the proceedings, waiting for her moment. I could see her hands shaking as she rose, clutching the account sheet like a lifeline as she spoke into the silence, every year the same words: 'I have audited the books and found them to be correct.' That was all and, though I sympathised with her feelings, I could never understand her problem or see it as anything but funny. Meanwhile, I was learning to speak in public myself.

The staff who had seen the High School through the war years were beginning to be replaced by younger women with fresh ideas and new enthusiasms. These encompassed the establishment of a Council for Education in World Citizenship (CEWC) group and a revitalised Debating Society, open to the Middle School. Though I never quite lost the same dislike of addressing an audience from cold which afflicted my mother, I joined both and grew to revel in discussion and thoroughly enjoy the meetings and debates. Above all, still unable to express my views freely at home without the threat of a row developing, I relished the opportunity to say what I thought about the issues of the day. Attitudes were changing faster than my father's strong opinions, which I was not expected to question. I remember that my choosing to speak against capital punishment in one of the debates did not go down well with him.

School was offering me other activities also, and extensions to existing ones. Both Hilary and I had become school librarians, eventually to take charge of the fiction library, newly housed in a room only big enough for a handful of people at a time, but an improvement on cardboard boxes and a cupboard in the gym. As a result we found ourselves making terrifyingly erratic journeys to Manchester as Mrs Johnson drove us to its bookshops to select new stock, but once we were there it was wonderful; books everywhere – and she bought us lunch. There were other trips from school, too, ranging from meetings with the CEWC to visits to the Town Hall to support our civics lessons, and theatre visits in connection with our English Literature course. One of those was to a performance of *Julius Caesar* at Blackpool Tower Circus, where the mournful ghost tripped up on the way across the arena. That did little for the dramatic impact of the play for an audience composed largely of schoolchildren.

But not everything was connected with politics or study. There were also outdoor activities. Though I enjoyed tennis, and not only because it enabled me to evade my father's vigilance and hang around with my friends at the tea bar in the pavilion at the top of the park, I was still not a games player. What attracted me was yet more walking, based on the school YHA group resurrected by a new games mistress. I joined immediately, as did Hilary, Enid and Hazel, who were by then my closest friends. So began a period of local walking and weekend excursions to Derbyshire, including something even I had never done before – a midnight hike.

It seemed strange to be setting out in the warm air of a scented summer evening, our shadows stretching ever longer behind us. We walked steadily from somewhere near Clitheroe, but midnight was almost upon us as we tracked across the moor below the summit of Gaughey Hill. A distant clock chimed as we began the steep descent to Slaidburn, carrying clearly across the valley. Below us, the elbow bend in the road above the village gleamed like bone in the light of a full moon.

Down we went and on, between hushed houses and past sleeping farms where dogs barked at our footsteps. Torches were redundant; stark shadows marked our way in black and white. As we climbed a stile a cow rose clumsily to her feet beside us, lowing in protest and making us laugh and turn up our noses at the animal smell as we moved by; shapes in the night, crossing fields and rough pasture in a dreaming world. I felt curiously distant, even in the midst of my friends. I had walked in the dark before, but never so late, never so far from settlements nor into the dawning day, as we did to reach our destination in the Trough of Bowland.

But I was doing too much. Something had to go. First were the Saturday morning art classes, then dancing. I still enjoyed it, but it was occupying a great deal of my time. Miss Boderke had been anxious for me to take the remaining exam, which would give me the teaching qualification she thought I should have, and rather reluctantly I agreed. I was her only candidate so one grey day, accompanied by both Miss Boderke and my mother, I boarded the train for Liverpool. I had been practising hard for weeks but it had been several years since my last exam. I was unenthusiastic and resigned rather than excited. Miss Boderke gave me reminders from time to time, 'Don't forget to turn your head. Remember to use your arms properly. Listen carefully. Answer the questions clearly,' but mostly she talked to my mother as I half listened, stared out at the dank countryside or read.

Lime Street Station seemed vast. It was crowded on our arrival and pushing our way through to the steps leading down from it, we found that it was raining hard. Not even Miss Boderke knew exactly where our destination was, just that it was a dancing school not far from the station which had been chosen as the regional examination centre that year. She pulled out the address and found someone to ask while Mother and I looked about us. 'Do you remember it?' she inquired. 'We came here years ago when we had runabout tickets and went for a ride on the Overhead Railway.'

'I remember being cold, and a great crowd of angry men, but not much else.'

'Yes, that was it. There was a dockers' meeting at Pierhead, and your father rushed us round them very quickly.'

'I don't remember any of this,' I added, gazing at the massive buildings around us, which looked dirty and uninviting in the pouring rain. 'I hope the exam's not in one of those.' It was not. It turned out to be on an upper floor of a far less imposing building overlooking a gloomy square and, as we mounted the worn stairs, my spirits declined yet more as nervousness took over. Meeting a smiling mother and daughter on their way down should have encouraged me, but it did not.

All too soon I was in a studio not too unlike the one I was used to, but bigger, feeling cowed by the businesslike severity of the ladies facing me across the bare expanse of floor. The greyness of the day outside had penetrated the room and the rain lashing against the grimy windows competed with their voices as I listened to my instructions. As the notes of the piano pierced the silence I began to dance, but hesitantly, unable to surmount my surroundings and lose myself in the familiar routines. Without rapport with an audience to release me I struggled through, coped with the questions and went home expecting a low pass. When the letter arrived to say I had failed I was upset, but not entirely surprised. Inevitably, it brought my dancing career to an end.

My activities in the Guides lasted a little longer – I had become Company Leader and was enjoying the responsibility – but by the time I took my GCE examinations I had resigned from that as well. I had, though, at last ventured onto the town's social scene in my first attendance at the Saturday night dance, having succeeded, with my mother's help, in wresting permission from my father.

I was so excited. Mother had made me a new dress. Light blue it was, in shiny taffeta with a woven leaf pattern, its stiffened three-tiered skirt held out by an even stiffer petticoat. Though I had recovered from the sort of embarrassment that had threatened to destroy my holiday in Minehead, I was not entirely comfortable with the deeply scooped neck, but otherwise I was delighted with the whole creation and had even made myself a matching handbag from some spare material. Silver dancing shoes, the crystal necklace and matching clip-on earrings Ian had once given me, a touch of eye shadow, a hint of lipstick plus a dab or two of my mother's powder, and my outfit was complete.

I had actually been out dancing a couple of times with Ian when he came north to visit his relatives, but to the Locarno Ballroom. Going without a partner to the youthful mecca of King George's Hall was an altogether different experience, an adventure. Questions swirled in my head. What would it be like? Would anyone ask me to dance? Would any of the boys I admired from afar be there? Would I meet someone new, someone special? I was dressed for the part. I felt good. I was ready.

I met Hilary by Victoria as usual, and in a very short time we were there, depositing our coats and outdoor shoes in the cloakroom and fitting the obligatory plastic caps to our stiletto heels. Then it was into the hall itself, startlingly unfamiliar. Gone were the rows of seats, those remaining lined up along the sides of the dimly lit auditorium in an ominous likeness to a dentist's waiting room. The hall seemed vast in its cleared emptiness, intimidating, the surrounding balcony rising into darkness.

We had arrived quite early and though there were scattered groups of boys and girls standing about as we hesitated near the doorway, not much seemed to be happening. I felt at a loss, not really knowing where to go or what to do, convinced that everyone was staring at us. I began to wonder if my neckline was too revealing after all, if my stocking seams were crooked. I was uncomfortable standing there and gladly followed Hilary across the floor to where we could be less conspicuous in two of the chairs. As we did so, the place was transformed. Without warning I found myself moving inside a kaleidoscope. I had no idea what was happening. Everywhere I looked patches of colour swirled silently around me, washing indifferently over walls, floor and people. Not until we had made it to the chairs could I locate the source and stare in wonder at the multi-faceted silver ball circling above my head.

The room was filling fast. Soon there were other girls and a few boys occupying chairs near us. Meanwhile, the groups on the floor had merged into a shifting whole, broken by dancers moving to the music which had started up when the lights had begun to gyrate, music which was new to me and set my feet twitching. I was excited again, full of anticipation. As I watched I was surprised to see that girls were dancing together, in groups or pairs, swinging each other about as I had watched my schoolfellows do in the gym, performing similar steps. I knew I could move to music, but swing and spin like that? And with Hilary? Never!

Sometimes boys broke briefly into the circles of girls, but generally they just stood around in the same way that Hilary and I were sitting. This was so far from what I had imagined. No longer supported by anticipation, my excitement waned. I sat there disconsolately, convinced that the place was not for me, wondering if Hilary would agree to go home and considering whether I could face the humiliation of returning early after all the fuss I had made. But then the music changed. Suddenly, the dancing was the ballroom that I knew.

This was better. Couples moved onto the floor as I waited expectantly for some one to invite me to dance. Waited and waited. No one did, neither me nor Hilary. Pretending not to mind, we contented ourselves with commenting on the people getting to their feet or dancing in front of us

'I wonder why he asked her? That green frock really doesn't suit her.'

'Yes, but her hair's lovely, nearly the same red as yours. Anyway, he can't dance. She's going to have very sore toes when he's finished.'

'Hey, there's John. I wonder if he'll come over?' Hilary waved to an acquaintance of hers who promptly turned away to his friends. Matters were not improving. Empty chairs now stretched away on both sides, isolating us.

'Let's go to the cloakroom,' I muttered, 'or get some lemonade or something,' but as I did so, one of a group who had been standing nearby for some time began to walk towards us. I could see him looking directly at me and smiled as I took in his smart sports jacket and neatly knotted tie. This is it, I thought. At last. Then he asked Hilary.

Sitting there on my own was agony, trying to look as if I didn't care. I did care, terribly, and was mortified by my confusion. Hilary was dismissive of her partner when she came back but that was no help; she had at least had one. The evening seemed to be going well for everyone else, full of music, movement, voices and laughter, but we sat pathetically on the sidelines as the long, humiliating moments shuffled by. I danced twice that evening, Hilary rather more, but those excruciating hours as the proverbial wallflower were the memory I came away with.

'Did you have a good time?' my father asked.

'It was OK,' I lied, 'but I don't think I want to go again for a bit.'

'Well, as long as you enjoyed yourself,' he replied, satisfied, but my mother gave me a very old-fashioned look when I sloped off to bed without telling her anything about it. I had suffered so much from embarrassment and humiliation that I never did go again, nor to any other public dance, unless I had a partner. In any case, as exams loomed closer, so other activities faded into the background.

I worked hard in my GCE year, resisting the calls of sun, friends and fresh air as I laboured over my books, struggling to retain the information I needed. It was as well I did, for a month or so before the exams my mother was called into hospital for a mastoid operation. She had been growing steadily more and more deaf in one ear, the result of a snowball incident in her childhood she claimed, and the time had arrived for something to be done about it. The very idea of my mother being in hospital terrified me. I felt again the sick horror I had experienced some years earlier on arriving home from school to find her being stretchered down the back steps to an ambulance after breaking her leg in a fall in the garden. She had been kept in for a time then, and I remembered the visiting: the cold, frightened flutter of my stomach as we went in, Mother in bed looking unfamiliar and out of place, echoing corridors and the repellent hospital spell. I remembered how she had feared for Mrs Ashton when she had a gall bladder operation, warning me that she might die. Now I feared for her.

By the time the exam period started towards the end of June she was back home, sadly unable to hear any better, but the whole episode upset my revision physically as well as emotionally. My father did his best, taking over the washing up and, since he fried his bacon rather than grilling it as my mother did, treating me to fried bread for breakfast, which I wolfed down between the house and the main road as I rushed off to school. However, he knew nothing of doing the washing or cleaning, and very little about cooking. His limits were a fry-up, pancakes – one of which he really did stick to the ceiling when he was showing off to me and David when we were little – and dabs. He cooked the latter so beautifully as to make the ones I sometimes bought from the chip shop seem like the work of amateurs, but Mother always prepared the batter for both of them.

Fortunately we had a washing machine by then, a Hoover twin tub. I had to remove the old mangle top which my father had fitted over it to provide a kitchen table before I could connect it to the sink taps, but at least I did not need to do the ordinary washing by hand. The sheets had to go to the self-service launderette which had opened in Victoria Street where, though I disliked the place, I could at least revise as I waited. Nevertheless, running the house, visiting the hospital and caring for and helping my mother when she returned home left little time for study. I never thought to mention my problems at school, only being told I should have done so when it was too late to write to the examination board. Perhaps a plea of extenuating circumstances might have earned me the extra five marks I needed to pass Latin – but perhaps not.

Far more significant to me at the time was the last blazing row I had with my father, over one of the maths exams. I had remained in the second division, to which I had been assigned following early problems with algebra, but with Miss Hindle's sympathetic support had become quite competent and had no fear of the exams. Mathematics, however, was one of the subjects my father taught at Blakey Moor. Over the years I had learnt that his ways of doing things were different, so had contrived to keep my maths homework well away from him unless I was desperate for help. Naturally, he was keen to discuss the first maths paper with me when I brought it home at lunch time. I should have left it at school.

'Looks all right. Which questions did you do?' I showed him without a qualm, being reasonably satisfied with my performance. I made my second mistake as I pointed to a calculus question.

'I wasn't too happy about that one.' Instantly, the inquisition began.

'What was your answer? How did you do it?'

'Well, I don't know. I can't remember the answer. I just did it.'

'But you must know how you did it.' His voice was rising and my mother intervened.

'Come on, Vic, leave her alone. She's done it and it'll be all right. Come and get your dinners, both of you. You'll be late back.' But he would not stop. He took the paper to the table and continued questioning me as we ate, telling me that the answers that I could remember were wrong, that I was stupid, had failed.

As he became angrier and angrier in his disappointment, so I became more and more upset. 'I'm not stupid,' I shouted. 'It's not all wrong. We just don't do things your way. Stop yelling at me.' It was the scene in Malham Youth Hostel all over again. Finally, sobbing uncontrollably I fled upstairs, pursued by my mother.

'Come on,' she said firmly. 'Stop this. You've got another exam this afternoon.' But I was hysterical and could not stop. Not only that, but as I sat hunched on my bed, her arm around my heaving shoulders, racked by sobs and beginning to feel sick, a stream of blood from my nose joined my torrent of tears.

Eventually I regained control of myself and stopped crying, but nothing I or my mother or father could do would stop the nosebleed. He had to go back to work; I had another exam at half past two. He went next door for help. The house had been untenanted for a long time after the Gills left but, fortunately for me, it was then occupied temporarily by a doctor as he and his wife waited for their new house to be built. I was wary of them because they had an Alsatian dog which chased the cat and had bitten me, but after this I forgave them everything. The doctor stopped my nosebleed, calmed me down, bundled me into his car and took me back to school in time for the exam. Fortunately again, it was English Literature, which never gave me any problems. I was soon away in ancient Rome with Julius Caesar, all else forgotten.

The end of the exams more or less coincided with the end of term. I handed in the requisite pre-addressed postcard for my marks, said goodbye to those of my friends who were among the 53 in my year leaving to go out to work, and that was that; another stage in my education completed. That I would stay on into the sixth form was never questioned, not even before my father had obtained his degree and accepted the lecturing post he was about to take up at Manchester College of Commerce that would make the finances easier. But now I had to earn some money for myself, not for essentials, but for a holiday.

During the summer term, rumours which had begun to circulate about a possible skiing trip to Switzerland had proved true. Though the school had run educational and cultural trips and exchanges over many years, this was a completely new and unheard of venture. I was as excited as everyone else by the rumours, delighted when it became known that it would be for fifth and sixth formers, and crestfallen when I saw how much it was going to cost. Wistfully I abandoned all thoughts of travelling abroad, but not so Enid. With the prospect of a career as a physical education teacher ahead of her, she was desperate to go and wanted me to go with her. Under her persuasion I finally mentioned it to my parents who, to my utter amazement, did not immediately dismiss the idea but started to consider the cost carefully and discuss it with Enid's parents. The answer came: if we could earn enough, we could go, but it would have to be done over the summer before numbers were finalised. Joyfully we celebrated that and the end of the exams with a day out in Southport on the first day of the holidays, then set about earning money.

On the strength of my years spent helping in the school library I went off to see the Chief Librarian in the public library, where I was still an avid borrower. To my delight he agreed to take me on for a week or two as holiday cover. Perhaps, though I did not see it at the time, it had something to do with the fact that his daughter had also put her name down for the trip.

Being a library assistant involved shift work and Saturdays, and included having to arrive long before the library was open to ensure that every book was shelved in its right place when it did, but I was happy with that. The cosy quiet of the book-filled room was a delight to me, but so was the lively companionship behind the issue desk where I spent most of my time. 'That will be threepence, please,' I said one morning, delving into the files to retrieve the library tickets for a prosperous-looking gentleman who was returning some overdue books.

'I'm on the Council,' was his response. Odd, I thought. Perhaps he was newly appointed and very proud of it or something. He was not the first borrower to make an unexpected remark and I had quickly learnt to make what I hoped was a pleasant response and pass on.

'That must be interesting,' I offered, still holding his tickets. 'Have you got the threepence, please?

'I'm on the Council,' he reiterated more firmly. This time I understood, and was disgusted.

'May I have the threepence, please?' I persisted, with a smile. As he paid up, took his tickets and left, I turned to find my colleagues spluttering with suppressed laughter.

Far less entertaining was the week I spent helping in the hairdressers at the bottom of Eanam where my mother and I were customers. Everything was fine until I was allowed to wash a client's hair prior to a perm. I was far too tentative about the whole business so the perm failed to hold and had to be redone for nothing. Thoroughly chastened, I was reduced to sweeping the floor and making tea, and my early departure at the end of the week was as much a relief to me as it was to the proprietor. It was a long time before I felt comfortable again just going for a hair cut.

Next, Alan's father took pity on me and invited me to help in his bakery. I was quite shocked to find that he started work every day at what I thought of as the middle of the night, and grateful that he did not expect me to do so. By the time I arrived, at about 8am, to start filling meat pies and icing buns, he had been in the back of his shop for hours baking the bread which I could smell as I approached, savouring the thought of the piece there would be waiting for me. He was tall and thin like Alan, but with gingery hair, a keen naturalist and a member of Blackburn Field Club as well as the Rambling Club, and so a great supplier of information on walks, as well as a great joker. I liked him and enjoyed myself at the bakery where he taught me a few tricks of his trade as well as paying me. 'Watch this,' he instructed, taking a small dollop of icing in one hand and a bun in the other. Then, like a conjuror, a flick of the knife, a twirl of the bun and there it was, perfectly iced.

The least enjoyable but the most lucrative of my jobs, serving refreshments in a hospitality tent at the agricultural show in Witton Park, was found for both of us by Enid. We thought it would be easy, just handing out refreshments without even having to take money, and that we would be able to see something of the show for nothing. How wrong we were. It was dreadful.

The real problem was the weather. The first day was fine so we were able to learn what we had to do, work without too much pressure and indeed take it in turns to slip out and watch what was happening, just as we had anticipated. After that it rained, almost continuously. Inevitably more and more guests crowded into our tent, seeking respite from watching the events in the ring or visiting the various stalls and displays. The tables never seemed to empty as we slithered over the increasingly muddy grass between them, whipping away cups and plates, wiping off crumbs, cutting more sandwiches and serving a seemingly endless soaking stream of new arrivals with steaming tea. Rain pounded on the canvas roof, rivulets ran down the walls and the atmosphere grew clammy and odorous, though the cheery visitors seemed not to mind. I did. The crowds thinned a little in the rare bright periods, but all that gave me was time to exchange a few words with Enid and realise just how much my feet hurt, my back ached and I longed to sit down. The pressure was awful, but the money was amazing; not because we were paid well, but because the tips were enormous. By the time the show was over I knew two things: that I would never again take a job in any form of catering, and that I would be able to make enough money to go to Switzerland.

Destination in View

In September 1956, the year of the first British nuclear power station, Britain's deportation of Archbishop Makarios from Cyprus and the Suez crisis with its attendant threat of nuclear strikes by Russia, I entered the Lower Sixth. Thirty-five of us, just over a third of the year, had elected to return to school, to be placed alphabetically into two forms for administrative purposes, but divided by our subject choices. Since I still had no particular career in mind, following my father's dictum I was doing more or less what I wanted, although I had rather reluctantly opted for French rather than art as likely to be more useful. Thus I was pleased when I was able to share with Enid the design and execution of the backdrop for the junior dancing display on Speech Day. I was even more pleased when the whole thing, a 12ft by 6ft representation of an open book with a nursery rhyme depicted on each of the two pages to support the dancing theme, was taken to the Children's Library and displayed there for several months.

I had no hesitation in choosing my other two subjects, Geography and English Literature. I was also studying O level German for fun, and retaking Latin, so had quite a heavy programme. Nevertheless it was a period of relative idleness as far as work was concerned as I, and most of my friends, relaxed after the pressures of the previous year. Having forsaken most of my out-of-school activities apart from the Rambling Club, and not being such a regular attendee even there, school and day-to-day outings with school friends became the focus of my life, foremost among them the ski trip.

Before long the group was finalised and details issued, including the extra clothing we would need. Waterproof trousers were on the list, together with anoraks, warm sweaters, thick socks and protective gloves. I had the socks, and the gloves would have to be bought, but for the rest it was back to knitting and sewing, starting with a trip to the market.

In the 1950s, Blackburn market consisted of three parts. The most obvious was an imposing stone market hall adjacent to the Town Hall, fronted by a clock tower on top of which a golden ball rose up a pole as 12 o'clock struck and down again at one, apparently to mark the dinner hour for workers without watches. When I was little I insisted on waiting for it if we were nearby. Unlike both the long, smelly tunnel of a fish market which ran alongside it and the open market, which were limited to three days a week, the Market Hall was open from Monday to Saturday and was the source of many of our supplies. My mother had her favourites among the rows of stalls which filled the lofty, tiled interior, some painted wooden lock-ups, others just boards with gaily striped awnings, and occasionally we patronised the tiny café for a cup of tea. More often, though, the drinking was restricted to my buying a glass of sarsaparilla from the adjacent stall as my mother queued to buy cheese, crumpets or soft oatcakes from her usual Preston stallholder. I always encouraged her to buy their floppy, oval oatcakes which I relished spread with jam for tea.

Where we bought our fruit and vegetables varied a little according to what was on display. Sometimes it was Harty's, sometimes Talbot's – owned by the occupant of No. 5 Whinfield Place, at the top of our garden – but more often Anelay's because Mother knew the proprietors better. There she could rely on not being given poorer goods from behind the attractive displays. Their daughter was in my year at school and whenever the morning hymn was *Eternal Father Strong to Save*, as I sang:

> *O hear us when we cry to thee*
> *For those in peril on the sea...*

I thought of her brother, as he was the only sailor I knew of.

Most of Mother's haberdashery and knitting needs were met by Dibdin's, in New Bank Road, or stalls in the covered market, but we needed material for my trousers and anorak so it was to the open market that we went. This was held on the ground surrounding the Market Hall, and the area alongside it, between the back of King William Street and Victoria Street. Sockets were sunk into the granite sets at regular intervals to take the corner posts of the dozens of close-packed stalls which sprang up in serried ranks three times a week, accompanied by much shouting, clattering and banging. They formed a grid of narrow streets with every conceivable household need enticingly displayed on wooden counters beneath tarpaulin roofs. On fine days it was a great place to go; bustling, colourful and friendly. It was impossible to spend long there without stopping to pass the time of day or exchanging gossip with an acquaintance in the throng.

Again Mother had her favourite stalls for various materials, but something waterproof was new, so some searching was necessary. Our first try was unsuccessful, partly because it was, appropriately, wet. The grey drizzle which threw into relief the dull illumination from the swinging light bulbs quickly drowned my enthusiasm as I followed her from stall to stall. Tired of dodging the rivulets of rain which the canvas roofs created, and of feeling the water dripping down my neck and bouncing back from the shimmering stones and puddles beneath my feet as I sloshed and wriggled my way through the damp crowds, I persuaded her to abandon the quest for another day. Meanwhile she sorted out patterns and checked the amounts she needed. Our next search for material was successful, and I was well on the way to having a navy blue anorak and trousers.

That left the thick sweater to make. This time I went looking for a pattern and found my dream garment. It was a zip jacket with a Fair Isle yoke and a matching bobble hat, the ideal thing, but far too complicated for me to knit in the time available. Yet another member of the Rambling Club, Mrs Chapman, came to the rescue. For a moderate sum she knitted not only my sweater but a similar one for Enid, in different colours. Our hats we knitted ourselves, the ability to make pom-poms with cardboard circles learnt at junior school coming in useful at last.

Buying the gloves was an event. Mother took me to The Glove Shop in King William Street, like Granville Fashions, the canopied dress shop in New Bank Road, the sort of prestigious establishment where I never expected to do more than look in the windows. Once she understood what we needed, the assistant delved into wooden drawers to produce various pairs of gloves and mittens, which she set out carefully on the glass-topped counter. I hardly dared touch them at first, but eventually selected a pair of red mittens, fitted with buckles to tighten the cuffs, to match the red in my sweater. Used to hand-knitted gloves, I could hardly believe that these were going to be mine. I unwrapped them on the bus on the way home, slipped them on and off and stroked the soft leather against my cheek as I inhaled the odour. Their price, however, reminded me that I had to earn more money.

My next scheme involved no more than sitting at home sewing, burning the fronts of my legs as I huddled by the fire. Mother had an original embroidered Rambling Club badge on her rucksack and was always being asked where they could be obtained. They could not, so I made a pattern from the existing one, sorted out some bits of material and embroidery threads of the right colour from her stocks and took orders. Unfortunately I underestimated the demand, so had to buy more thread and spend too many long autumn evenings stitching furiously to fulfil them.

The badges were almost my last venture. Only working on the Christmas post remained, for which I was at last old enough. I was not accepted to do deliveries, a task which paid better and was mostly done by boys, but I knew I would earn enough and was not anxious to lug heavy bags round the streets or face fierce dogs. I was content to spend the week in the sorting office, frantically thrusting envelopes into multiple rows of pigeonholes in the battle to have all the mail sorted and despatched before everything closed down late on Christmas Eve. Only as I left the silent hall, the lines of cleared pigeonholes and the rapidly emptying building, did I have a moment to think of other things. As I stepped out into a deserted Darwen Street I wanted to shout my joy to the heavens; in a week I would be in Switzerland.

The ski trip left Blackburn on 28 December, our orange luggage labels fluttering in the breeze to complement the badges we were sporting as we gathered at the railway station. Our first stop was London, exciting enough in itself. Being crammed into cramped accommodation in a small hotel near Victoria Station did nothing to dampen my delight. This was me, in the capital for the first time in my life, and furthermore we four members of the Lower Sixth were off to traverse it on our own. The main party were going to see *The Reluctant Debutante* at the Cambridge Theatre, but we had been accorded the privilege of selecting our own entertainment. After much investigation and discussion we had made our choice, sent our postal order to the Keith Prowse booking agency – my task – and were now on our way to the Ambassadors' Theatre, carefully carrying our tickets for Agatha Christie's *Mousetrap*, in the first month of its fifth year. As I descended a dusty flight of steps to the challenge of the Tube, my friends beside me, I experienced an inexpressible surge of joy and excitement.

The following day saw us crossing from Folkestone to Calais by breezy ferry. Never having been in anything bigger than a rowing boat, Enid and I investigated everything and I was amazed when I opened a door in the bowels of the ship to find railway lines with carriages standing on them. Then came our night train to Basel and trying to sleep on the hard, dark green leatherette couchettes. I woke once at a station to hear a voice shouting something like Amyan, Amyan. Peering out round the blind to the dimly lit platform I read 'Amiens', and knew myself truly abroad. On the rack and pinion railway from Martigny to Les Marecottes, our final destination, I could hardly bear to turn from the window. As we climbed beneath a blazing blue sky, from green, chalet-strewn valleys through snow-laden trees towards snowy slopes and distant peaks, my dreams were materialising before me.

Our accommodation, which we and our luggage finally reached by jeep from the station, I had not visualised. Enid and I clattered up the stairs to find our low, eaves-darkened room mostly occupied by a large, wooden framed bed which we were clearly to share, though we could hardly see it for the white cloud of coverlet which seemed to have settled over it. As we clomped around on the uneven wooden floor, investigating everything, flinging open the windows onto the tiny balcony and stuffing our clothes into the heavy, carved furniture, we were pleased to discover it was actually two beds in one, though we remained bemused by the bolsters and absence of blankets. We had yet to discover the bliss of being enveloped in the feathery lightness of the billowing white quilts, which hung like bunting from the village balconies and windows every morning.

Once we had collected our long, wooden skis and the peculiar leather boots with notches in the heels to hold their wires, our days fell into a pattern. In the mornings came our skiing lessons: hours of fun as we floundered, fell and finally acquired enough skill to take the lift and move up the mountain. There I thrilled to the swish of my skis cutting snow, the harmonic motion of twists and turns and the effortless descents, like dancing on the landscape. In the afternoons we were free to do as we pleased. Sometimes we practised in groups, sometimes we tramped the crisp, white trails around the village. I was used to snow, but not to snow glittering in sunlight from an azure sky, softening the silence of scented forests, enfolding picturesque chalets and dressing the slopes of mighty mountains, one of which, Le Luisin, I would eventually return to and climb. The landscape, the air, had a magnificence, a cleanliness and freshness I had never known, and I exulted in it.

Since the village offered little in the way of shops, Enid and I decided to spend one afternoon sledging the five miles down the quiet, snow-clad road to Martigny to buy presents, but first we had to hire a toboggan. Since no one in the village spoke English it fell to me, struggling with A level French, to make the first attempt. '*Bonjour, Monsieur. Nous voulons louer une luge,*' I tried, my words sort of French, my accent definitely Lancashire. The proprietor shrugged and looked blank. I tried again, but the stalemate only ended when Enid produced her purse and pointed.

Pleased with ourselves, we climbed aboard and pushed off. However, we had failed to appreciate that it had thawed as well as snowed since our arrival. A mile below the village we ran out of snow, but undeterred we dragged our transport the rest of the way. By the time we had done that and bought our presents, darkness had fallen, but an area of the town towards which people were drifting seemed brightly lit and noisy. Curious, we followed, and so became spectators as Martigny's last tram began its final journey through the streets, to the accompaniment of bands and waving flags. Our journey then was less ceremonious: a run with our toboggan to catch the train which would deliver us to Les Marecottes for our evening meal, to be followed by socialising in the café with other visitors. As usual, on our way there we paused by the rickety fenced ice rink where the hiss of skates and shouts of skaters rang out in the cold starlight. I had declined to take the slightly mildewed skates my mother had ferreted out from under our stairs, but standing there I regretted it. Without skates I could only watch, and I wanted to skate.

The entire trip was tremendous until the final day. On almost my last descent I ran straight into deeper snow, my skis crossed and I flew over them. The rest is confusion. I looked at my leg and saw, or thought I saw, my foot facing backwards; I could hear screaming, realised it was me and tried to stop; saw the ski instructor racing towards me; felt him releasing my skis – then nothing. My next clear memory is of lying in bed in the hotel with a desperately painful and heavily bandaged knee, having returned from hospital. But I was not the focus of attention; Enid was. She lay moaning and writhing in agony in the other half of the bed, watched by anxious looking staff as they waited for the doctor. I made it back to England but she did not, or not for another two weeks, which she spent in hospital having had her appendix removed. On my return I found being unable to bend my knee and so having to stand in assembly like a lighthouse when the rest of the school knelt to pray almost as bad as the pain. Though I skied again I was always wary of it, but not of foreign travel.

I had opted for A level geography partly because I enjoyed the outdoors and seeing other places. Going to Switzerland showed me that this could apply to the world. David was still in Hong Kong, sending letters and garish, hand-coloured postcards depicting a place full of colour and vitality, teeming with tiny people overlooked by illuminated Coca-Cola signs as big as the buildings they were attached to. As we studied South-East Asia, his words brought a different dimension to the black-and-white images which broke up the text of my dilapidated geography book where farmers in lampshade hats drove oxen through soggy fields. I wanted to see things for myself. As Miss Seed, another of our new breed of post-war teachers with up-to-date knowledge and modern ideas, talked about the teeming Chinese and prophesied the future prominence of their nation, I dared to dream that one day I, too, might go there. But even I did not envisage another area of our studies as a potential destination. As Fuchs and Hillary made the first crossing of Antarctica we plotted their progress, studied reports, articles and photographs and discussed their dangers and difficulties, and I was both enthralled and appalled by their exploits.

Meanwhile, I had to content myself with the only field trip our class of six ever made, to Borrowdale in the Lake District. Hardly comparable, but we enjoyed it as we paired off to study various aspects of the valley on a sunny, crisp February weekend, gathered to discuss our findings informally in the evenings and then mix with the crowd in the hostel. Hazel and I, set to investigating settlements, identified a rapidly declining population, particularly in Grange where, memory tells me, we found only seven male inhabitants.

By then I had my own ideas about some of the social and political questions of the time, which I discussed endlessly with my friends. Capital punishment, not abolished until the mid-1960s, was still on our agenda, as were the Suez crisis, the Cyprus problem and the threat of nuclear war. I particularly regretted the fact that my scholarship English lessons precluded my attendance at the headmistress's philosophy class the day she criticised the newly launched CND. One of my normally reticent classmates, whose father was an avid member and marcher, exploded into speech, and I would have enjoyed the subsequent debate.

I was, however, fortunate enough to be one of the team which joined the Grammar School on a trip to Granada Studios to take part in *Youth Wants to Know,* a series in which we interviewed Field Marshal Sir John Harding on his return from his post as Governor of Cyprus. My question was not one of the six selected, but being there with someone so important was a real thrill. My proud parents, who went to Aunty Jessie's to watch the programme, did at least catch a glimpse of me.

At about the same time, two or three of us set out to heckle Barbara Castle, who was holding an evening meeting by the side of the fish market. Since she was immensely popular there was quite a crowd surrounding her raised platform, but we could see and hear her easily from our position slightly behind them. Eventually one of our group, probably Caroline or Hilary, certainly not me, called out an objection to something she said. Mrs Castle responded and seemed not to mind, but the crowd did. Heads turned, people shuffled, glared and muttered.

'Cheeky kids!' I heard.

'Where are your manners?'

'Clear off.'

In the gloom, it was almost frightening. Also, as sixth formers, we were no longer bound by the rule that banned uniform in town without permission or an accompanying parent, so could easily be identified. Though it would be three years before we were old enough to vote, we still slipped away annoyed at being dismissed as children, as we considered ourselves quite mature. After all, some of our discussions were now held over coffee in town centre cafés on Saturday mornings, where we were served at cloth-covered tables by white-pinafore clad waitresses. Our favourite venue for a time was the Cinema Royal, but we were also regulars at Booths, the first café that the Blackpool grocery chain opened, above what was its fifth shop on the market corner of King William Street, and at the superior County Café opposite. Still an avid reader, I normally linked these gatherings to visiting the library. On fine days I walked back home through Corporation Park, often stopping to read in the Memorial Garden, drawn by the background of fountain and birdsong.

I had not lost my love of being outside and continued to go walking, sometimes with the flourishing school YHA group with which I first climbed Kinder Scout one weekend, with the Rambling Club and with my schoolfriends. I enjoyed the planning of our own trips almost as much as the trips themselves, leafing through the YHA handbook to choose hostels and check the distances between them, planning the routes and then finding the way. Very different, however, were the weeks I spent near Elterwater with Enid and Hazel, and two or three others, when invited by one of our teachers to assist Mr W.O. Bell, then Chief Education Officer for Birmingham, who regularly took parties of disadvantaged youngsters to the Lakes at Easter. There was no danger of my refusing the offer of a free week's holiday in exchange for helping others to climb mountains and enjoy what I enjoyed, and indeed I went twice. It was wonderful; Striding Edge, Great Gable, Helvellyn – a different mountain every day, and so much achievement, epitomised by the phenomenal feat of two blind girls who made it to the top of Scafell Pike. They could not see it but they knew they had climbed to the highest point in England, and I felt privileged to share their joy.

The week was not all walking. We stayed at the former Pillar Hotel on the Langdale Estate, the main party accommodated in the house, our teaching staff in the gatehouse and we volunteers in log cabins by the tarn. We had plenty of time to ourselves and group activities in the evenings, including a campfire and singing. On the final night our teachers invited us to join them for a drink in the pub in Chapel Stile. I was ridiculously excited and a shade apprehensive as we walked up the deserted road, grateful that my father was at least 100 miles away. In a shadowy corner of the cosy bar, shrouded in tobacco and woodsmoke, just 17 and very conscious of being under age, I gleefully sipped a glass of cider. For the first time in my life I was out for a drink.

By no means all my energies in the sixth form were devoted to the outdoors. I also had my first and last acting experience. In playing the small part of Grumio in a version of *The Taming of the Shrew* performed by members of VIB on the stage of Trinity Methodist Hall next door to the school, I concluded that my role in the theatre would be that of spectator. I thoroughly enjoyed the whole experience, including renovating the stage and building the set, and we went on to win a cup in the annual drama festival with one of the scenes, but I saw that it was not for me. I had no flair and found learning the lines difficult, though I continued to enjoy the Play Reading Society, which was enhanced by being one of the activities shared with the Grammar School.

Badminton, played in the gym above the stables at Crosshill, was another new activity, also shared with the Grammar School Sixth Form for doubles matches. Several of the group, both boys and girls, were my old St Silas' friends, so lived near by. After the matches we strolled to the end of Crosshill Road and stood around chatting before we parted, an innocent pleasure which resulted in my father's final attack on my behaviour. When he accepted his lectureship in Manchester he negotiated a system whereby he had Fridays off, but worked in the evenings on some of the days he was there. Thus he regularly returned home late, and on one occasion he spotted me from the bus. When I pranced in cheerfully some time later, he was waiting for me.

'Where've you been?' His tone was a little disconcerting, but I knew of no crime.

'Playing badminton. We won!'

'You weren't playing badminton when I saw you. You were hanging about with some boys at the end of St Silas' Road.'

'They were just the badminton team, Dad. And you know most of them.'

'I don't care. I'm not having a daughter of mine hanging around on street corners at 10 o'clock at night. If I catch you again, it'll be the last badminton you play.' This time, as my brother had done before me, I kept quiet as he ranted on and made sure he never caught me again. But his reprimand was in any case milder, and when the sixth form dance took place, his attitude surprised me.

I had fallen out with Alan. We were both retaking Latin and our deteriorating relationship had finally collapsed over a disagreement about using the pluperfect tense to put an English sentence into Latin. Thus I was unescorted, but I knew lots of people who would be there and saw it as an opportunity to make new friends. By the end of the evening I had indeed met a stranger, another Ian, who wanted to take me to the pictures. This was wonderful, a dream turned into reality. Confessing that I would have to ask my father who, like many others, was waiting outside, I hesitantly introduced him, expecting that to be the end of all my hopes. But I was wrong. My father approved, and the following Saturday became the focus of my life. I dreamt through lessons, held imaginary conversations and despaired over my paltry wardrobe as sleep evaded me. The week fizzed by in a frenzy of excitement which I tried my best to hide. The day came, and there he was, waiting for me by Victoria as I got off the bus.

My rehearsed words evaporated instantly, but Ian kept the rather strained conversation going as we walked through Salford and along Ainsworth Street to the Royal. At first the film could have been blank for all I knew, concerned as I was with my companion and the situation, but gradually I became so absorbed that it was a shock when I felt Ian's arm slide round me in the darkness. I had experienced that before, at times impatiently shrugged off invading hands and arms, not even interested in experimenting. My mother had either been too embarrassed to talk to me about the facts of life or assumed that my friends or the school would explain things to me, but neither had. No one did before I reached university. All I knew for certain was that if I kept my clothes on I would not become pregnant and have to leave school and marry the father, so bringing shame and disgrace to my family. This time, however, I feared that my advance decision to say no in the face of future temptation might be tested. Ian's arm lay there, searing my shoulders. I found myself responding, feeling the hairs on my neck tingle. It was thrilling, disturbing – and too good to last. During the interval between the B movie and the main feature, and on the way back to the Boulevard, it became obvious that we had little in common. We parted amicably, but with no plans to meet again.

All too soon, I had other things to think about. Exams were looming again, but first there came the question of what to do after them. Though on this occasion our parents were invited to school to discuss our futures – a rare event which I viewed with horror – I can remember no real careers guidance at all. For arts students like me the recommendation was teaching, for which the next step was two years at a teacher training college. Otherwise, it seemed, I might become a nurse or work in an office. I was not happy with that, and nor was my father. By then part way through an external law degree to add to his BSc, he suggested a career in law. That appealed to me, but his visit to school was the end of it. My old adversary, my Latin teacher, dismissed the idea completely on the basis of my problems with her subject – though I had by then passed it – so it was back to teaching. Since my father enjoyed his job and I liked school that seemed to make sense, but at the same time I wanted a wider experience before I committed myself. Though 19 of my classmates went to teacher training colleges, I never considered it. I wanted to try for university. The choice of subject was more difficult as I preferred Geography but was better at English. Geography won.

Lack of guidance let me indulge my fancy in wasting my first choice on Oxford. Turned down outright by Manchester, which I considered an affront, I was left with University College London, Liverpool and Sheffield. London was the first place to offer me an interview, so restoring my ego a little, and I waited impatiently for the day to arrive.

By the time my train reached Euston my excitement had declined, and with it had gone much of the meagre store of confidence it had been supporting. This continued to empty itself onto the pavements of Marylebone Road and Gower Street as I hunted for the entrance to University College. By the time I had passed through the imposing entrance, further awed by the figure manning it who was sporting a uniform which looked to me like fancy dress, I had little left. Hesitantly I approached the desk, followed the directions I was given for the room I wanted and seated myself on a hard chair outside it, with no more than a side glance and a muttered greeting towards the girl already sitting there, who was clearly another candidate. We hardly spoke. The uneasy silence lengthened until, apart from the absence of moaning and wailing from behind the closed door opposite, it began to feel to me like another nightmarish trip to the school dentist. I jumped in the heavy silence as the door opened. A boy left and my companion was ushered inside. Now I was alone, twiddling my clammy fingers in my lap, feeling more and more uncomfortable in the bare corridor and wishing I had never applied for this massive, seemingly soulless establishment.

It seemed a long time before my erstwhile companion emerged. She looked pleased. 'It was OK,' she murmured as she disappeared, but I was not encouraged. Another nerve-wracking wait until, finally, it was my turn.

'Miss Ryan?' inquired the lady as she opened the door. That instantly increased my confusion. I almost failed to recognise myself. It was the first time anyone except my friends, who called me anything from Joey to Rycan, despite my mother having deliberately given me a name she thought people could not tamper with, had addressed me as anything but Joan. I followed her into the room and closed the door as she resumed her seat next to a sombre-looking gentleman on the far side of a long table. Crossing what seemed like an acre of carpet I paused by the single chair on my side of the table. One of the few instructions I had been given – along with knock firmly but gently on the door, which I had not been in a position to do; smile, which in my nervousness I was struggling with; and tell the truth, which I would have done in any case – was not to sit down until invited to do so. Thus I hovered there, feeling ever more foolish.

'Do sit down!' It was the gentleman this time, barely glancing at me as he shuffled the papers in front of him, 'You're from Blackburn, I see.'

'Yes.'

'Which is where, exactly?'

'Lancashire.'

'And why do you want to come to London?'

Silence. This was almost, but sadly not quite, one of the imagined questions to which I had been mentally rehearsing answers throughout my long journey. Why London University, yes; why London, no! I struggled to rearrange my thoughts.

'Because it's the capital,' I began.

'Speak up.' It was the lady interrupting. If I ever knew her name I cannot recall it, and though I remember the cold austerity of the situation being broken by a shaft of sunlight reminding me that there was a free world outside, I left the room eventually with no recollection of what either of the interviewers looked like.

'Because it's the capital…' I tried again more loudly, but went stumbling on, completely without enthusiasm or conviction, and so it was with question after question, all of which seemed designed to unbalance me. Indeed, back at school the following day when I reported on the interview, my geography teacher was critical of both my treatment and the questions, but I suppose it must have been the same for everyone. I was just unable to cope with it. As the questions became more subject-based, so my answers became a little more fluent, but by then I was miserably convinced that the session was no longer anything more than an agonising formality which had to be endured. Despair displaced nervousness and I simply gave up.

Dismissed at last, I fled through the musty corridors to the haven of the noisy, dusty, sunlit street. Not until then, as I walked unheedingly towards the city centre, did the full import of my situation strike me and my struggle against tears begin. But it was not a struggle against tears of disappointment, that came later, but of anger and frustration at my own failure. Hot with shame and embarrassment, completely unable to reconcile myself to my own behaviour, I could only review my despicable performance and hate myself for it. As I walked the scene replayed itself over and over again in my imagination, questions whirled in my head and with them what I could have, should have, said. I tormented myself with the belief that I had thrown away my remaining chance of a place at a prestigious university in an exciting city, would be a disappointment to my parents and my school, and indeed might not get to university at all. Now I only had Liverpool, a city I did not much care for, or Sheffield, which I had never even seen. Would either of them take an idiot like me? Did I even want to go there? The tears began to win. I felt exposed, stupid, convinced that people were staring at me, so sought the relative obscurity of a side turning. I wanted somewhere to hide, to sit for a while and recover, but found no refuge in the blocks of blank buildings. On I went, giving way to my grief on the deserted pavements.

Once the tears had come and gone, with too much time wasted and little heart left for my intended sightseeing, I found my way back to Euston. Lonely and miserable, I escaped into the pages of my library book as the train carried me home to await what I knew would be my letter of refusal. Many years later, when I gained a library qualification at the same college, my success felt all the sweeter for the earlier experience.

Sheffield was next. Since it was a shorter, cheaper journey, and London had been so disastrous, my mother accompanied me. We spent several happy hours investigating the shops and sights of the compact city centre before I disappeared into the red brick recesses of Western Bank, and she into the sunny park next door to wait for me. Having practised in London I coped much better with the interview, so was quite cheerful as I rejoined her. Only time prevented me from taking her out in one of the rowing boats she had been idly watching on the small lake.

Liverpool offered another opportunity for a shared day out, but the city lived up to my image of it. It was again a grey day, windy and cold. Though the former dwelling house in Abercromby Square where I was interviewed was comfortable, and the interview itself by far the most pleasant and interesting of the three, I found the surroundings uninviting. The grass of the railed area where my mother huddled on a bench waiting for me struggled for survival, the few people about looked chilled and miserable, and bleak buildings and weed-filled bomb sites sprawled dismally into the distance as we made our way back to the station.

Interviews over, and not turned down by Sheffield or Liverpool, all I had to do was pass the exams. So came another season of study. Determined to succeed, I stayed in when my parents went out, buried myself in my bedroom with my books or took them with me when I sat in the sun. Meeting friends meant discussing work as we tried to make up for earlier idleness and keep up with our lessons. The arrival of the exams was a relief. This time there were no problems at home to upset me. I completed the papers and returned to school to await the end of term and my celebratory YHA trip to the Yorkshire Dales with Hilary.

On my last day at school I was as excited as anyone else, sharing in the chatter and laughter that filled our form room with increasing volume as we waited for our final assembly.

'No more school!' someone shouted.

'No more homework!'

'No more uniform!' Then sense became buried in a babble of sound. We were not to know that within 10 years our traditional school would be obliterated in the eruption of comprehensive education. Nor could we foresee that in 20 years hippies and skinheads would already have succeeded feuding mods and rockers; in 30, we would be shopping in supermarkets and dining in MacDonald's or foreign restaurants opened to serve returning package holidaymakers; in 40, a majority would have their own homes, cars and colour televisions; and in 50, the use of credit cards, mobile phones and the internet would be the norm. As the British Empire collapsed around us in Macmillan's 'you've never had it so good' Britain of teenage culture, unrationed goods, growing consumerism and developing technology, we saw only the changes in our own lives, not the accelerating pace of social change which was carrying us with it, trampling the world we had known.

I hardly heard the bell to bring us to order, but by the time we reached the lower corridor the racket had subsided so that only our footsteps competed with the music as we filed to the back of the hall, passing the assembled school for the last time. Miss Armstrong spoke a few sobering words concerning our imminent departure before wishing us well and praying for us, but otherwise the assembly was much like any other: coughing, shuffling, dust drifting in sunlight. Only as we rose from our knees to sing the end of term hymn, *Lord dismiss us with thy blessing*, for the 21st and final time, our feet scraping on worn wood, the honours boards above our heads a silent testament to those who had gone before, did I fully appreciate the finality of the occasion. Never again, I thought, never again, and found the solemnity of the moment and the words I was singing banished in a surge of exhilaration. Thus I was all the more surprised when we reached '*those who here shall meet no more*' to notice girls beside me beginning to weep.

I stood there, feeling slightly guilty and trying to justify my lack of emotion, until I caught Hazel's eye. She, who later marked the occasion by gathering up all her gym knickers and burning them in their Aga, smiled conspiratorially, as did Hilary, who skimmed her hat into the middle of the duck pond on her way home through the park. Yes, we were going our separate ways: to work, courses, training colleges and, for a privileged 10 of us, probably university, but we expected to remain in touch with our close friends and see them at Christmas. I was ready to move on, to leave my childhood behind me. I had yet to learn that it would never leave me.

Awaiting the Signal

Once released from the grip of exams, apart from my brief trip with Hilary I did none of the things I had promised myself I would do in my eight weeks of freedom. Instead, I found a job in a local footwear factory, and otherwise reverted to a more normal way of life. I also made time to visit Uncle Frank and Aunty Mary, no longer in Houghton but far away in Prescot, and with a third son I hardly knew. Going there made me realise how much I had missed them, but the overtime I was working still kept me away. No longer assuming that anyone having an operation would probably die, even when I heard that my uncle was going into hospital with a stomach ulcer, I remained at home. I did not visit them again until David, not long back from Hong Kong, came home on leave. Then we all went, though aware that Uncle Frank was still in hospital.

It was a long, hot journey on countless stifling buses as the landscape shimmered in August heat. Despite enjoying my brother's rare company, I was particularly glad to arrive and rather put out to see that Mary had a visitor. She was entertaining a tired-looking, painfully thin person, who remained seated, but smiled as we entered to fill the space around him. As I waited to be introduced, my father's words blasted my brain like bullets. 'Aren't you going to say hello to your uncle, Joan? How are you feeling, Frank?' Confusion gave way to horror as realisation dawned. A dreadful stillness gripped me as I fought for control, forced myself to move forward, smile, murmur a greeting and embrace the emaciated figure. I could not believe what my mind was telling me.

Throughout the afternoon David managed to join in the conversation, but I took refuge in playing with my cousins. From time to time I glanced covertly at the man in the chair, seeking some resemblance between him and the burly, cheerful uncle I loved. I could see none. Only his weakened voice held any likeness. Around me the room, the house, breathed sickness and sorrow, and I escaped gratefully with my brother when it was proposed that we take the children out before tea while Aunty Mary helped Uncle Frank to bed.

I remember little of the evening beyond the journey home. Though now four, and no dog, we spread ourselves along the front seat of the double-decker as we always had, but silent in our shared grief.

'I feel sick,' I whispered to David, as the bus bore us through the blackness.

'So do I,' he replied.

I had known nothing about cancer until then. The very word was taboo, the disease hushed up. Had my father known that his brother was in the house that day he would not have taken us, but Mary had only been expecting him so said nothing. Following an exhausting trip to Lourdes which had produced no miracle cure, Uncle Frank had chosen to leave hospital and return home to die. None of us saw him again.

My father's grief at his brother's death was paralleled by his concern for Mary and her three children, the oldest seven and the youngest not yet two. Having just about finished bringing up his own family, he automatically assumed responsibility for his brother's. Since they were obliged to vacate the police house they were occupying it was decided that they would return to Clitheroe, but Mary was in desperate need of help and support from my unhappy parents. I had never known our home so cheerless. The spring left my father's step and my mother ceased to whistle and sing in the kitchen. David returned to his unit and I, grieving in private, returned to my nightmares. Once again the fiendish cats threatened me from the stairs but worse, night after night I woke, or dreamt I woke, conscious of my surroundings but cold and rigid, my body refusing to obey my mind's instructions. I lay there, seized by terror, unable to move so much as an eyelid until, eventually, kind sleep reclaimed me.

In the midst of our misery, my father went out and bought a car. He knew nothing about vehicles, could not drive and for months had been failing to persuade my mother that we should get one. One morning he simply disappeared with Uncle Billy and returned with a decrepit tourer. Mother was horrified and grumbled for days, claiming that we could not afford it, that it took up too much room under the shed, that it was in the way of the washing, that there was no point in a car that no one could drive, that it was a wreck and would never run properly and that she, for one, was not going to clean it. She came round in the end, though not about the cleaning, and at least it gave us something else to think about.

I was highly entertained by my father's uncharacteristic action and supported him from the start, foreseeing a time when we might speed down the country's first stretch of motorway, the Preston bypass, then two months from its opening. Meanwhile, if we needed to move the car, my father pushed while I steered. Though the rag and bone man still came down the lane with his horse and cart calling his wares, car ownership had become so common that some of my friends, including Hilary, would be driven to their colleges and universities, but not me. It would be over 12 months before I motored over the Pennines, and then it would be on my second-hand Vespa scooter, which was as bad a bargain as my father's car.

In fact I was still not sure that I would be going to university, an anxiety not relieved until the release of the results and the subsequent offer of a place from both Liverpool and Sheffield. The probability of a better course in a city which had never shown me its attractive side lost out to the lure of a smiling Sheffield, with its easy access to the Peak District I had grown to love. However, by the time I made my decision, the 50 or so places in the women's hall of residence had been allocated and the best of the approved lodgings taken so when, after a great deal of correspondence, my parents and I returned to the city to inspect the most likely property, it was to the outlying district of Pitsmoor that we went.

I was unimpressed as the tram trundled its way through the sooty city, across the factory-fringed Don and up through the steep streets of a grinding hill, but the area proved to be more attractive than its name suggested. As we stood uncertainly at the tram stop I could see that the collection of shops on the other side of the road included at least a post office and a barber's which advertised women's haircuts. There appeared to be a small park beyond them too, but before I could see more my father found his place on my map, led us into Firshill Avenue, which turned out to be a cul-de-sac of large Victorian houses on the brow of the hill, found the right number and rang the bell.

The door was opened by a bustling Yorkshire lady of about my parents' age, who greeted us warmly.

'Good afternoon. Mr and Mrs Ryan is it, and?'

'Joan,' I supplied.

'Come along in. Did you have a good journey? What a long way. You'd like a cup of tea I expect, or would you like to have a look round first? Perhaps that would be best.' We agreed that it would, and followed her upstairs. 'Now this is the living room, with a coal fire at the end there. Mr Highton looks after that, and locking up and so on, and I serve the meals at the table here. That's breakfast and evening meal on weekdays and lunch as well at the weekends. There's a kitchen here for you to make drinks, but you'd need to bring your own mug' she went on, opening another door, 'and just the two bedrooms. There'll be two second years in this one. They were here last year, and you, Joan, would be sleeping in here with two other freshers.'

'Do you know who?' I managed to ask before she continued, but she did not.

'Now you'll want to think about it, so I'll just go and make that tea while you have a look round yourselves. Come down when you're ready.'

'Well,' my father began, once we had wandered rather aimlessly around the rooms again, 'what do you think?'

'She's a bit exhausting, but she seems very nice, and it it's all very clean,' my mother offered. He turned to me, already grinning at the thought of taking of another step towards my new existence. Apart from the distance from the city centre and the university, which was unavoidable, I could see nothing wrong with it. I nodded.

'Yes, it's fine,' and our conference was over.

'Right then. Let's see if we can settle it. But I need to know what she charges first.

My father was content with Mrs Highton's £5 per week, term-time only, and the deal was done. Ironically, the better job he had held for two years, from which the increased salary might have helped to pay for my education, simply reduced the amount of my means-tested grant. Though the town paid all tuition fees, he was expected to make up the difference between what I was allowed as living expenses and the value of a full grant, and I was well aware that he could not afford it. I did not need his grumbles at a system that allowed people with more money but less transparent earnings to obtain full grants for their children while he had to pay, to know that I had to spend as little as I could.

With gathering haste the preliminaries were completed. Mother and I went to Woolworths to choose mugs and glasses for my space in the kitchen; I treated myself to my first radio with some of my shoe factory earnings; my father took me to the Midland Bank to open an account and showed me how to write cheques, though I kept my post office account so I could draw money out anywhere; and I packed his wooden-bound, wartime trunk with my meagre possessions, including the blazer from which I had unpicked the school badge to be replaced with a university one when I arrived. As I stashed and folded I paused to admire my few new garments, though still wishing I had a coat to replace my school gabardine. When it was all done I watched with an uneasy feeling of finality as my belongings bounced away down the lane on the back of a British Railways flatbed lorry.

In the meantime, I had studied my information and instructions from the university until the edges were frayed, and made a provisional list of the societies I thought I might join. My violin, badminton racquet and walking boots were going with me, while the Officers' Training Corps figured high on my list of possible new activities. Under the continuing threat of nuclear war I wanted to be prepared – and had not failed to notice that signing on would not only give me lots of outdoor activity, but also some income and free driving lessons.

The weeks whirled by like falling leaves as summer faded, sweeping me with them; into town for last-minute purchases, to my friends' houses to say goodbye, to Clitheroe to see Mary and the boys, to Aunty Jessie's to part from Christine and her parents. And gifts came too: a leather briefcase from my father, an alarm clock from my mother, a picture from Mrs Ashton, and I was surprised and delighted when David arrived home unexpectedly with a hair dryer for me. The interest, the attention and my own nervous excitement were overwhelming. October arrived in a final flurry. Time to go.

It was raining when I left Blackburn. My father had already gone to work and was to meet me at Manchester Victoria and see me off on the Sheffield train from London Road. My mother had come to the station with me. As I waited for her to purchase a platform ticket, I gazed out through the drips from the booking hall canopy onto the familiar, bustling, rain-blurred boulevard which had witnessed so many of my comings and goings. For the first time I was not sure when I would return, and I was suddenly sobered by an unheralded flaring of affection for everything I was leaving, tinged with an inexplicable sense of loss. But not for long. Full of excitement, and happy in the belief – misplaced, of course – that I was fully equipped to cope with whatever my new existence might bring, neither the dismal weather nor the whisper of regret could depress my spirits, diminish my joy at making university, or dull my vision of a glittering, fun-filled future. I turned away readily as my mother rejoined me, and headed eagerly for the ticket barrier.

The train was already steaming away in the platform as we emerged from the subway, and I soon selected a compartment.

'This'll do,' I announced, putting my case down and opening the door. 'It's not for long anyway.'

'Are you sure you've got everything? You won't be allowed home for a bit, remember.'

'Well if I haven't, it's too late now. And anyway, you are going to visit me, aren't you?' The platform was emptying rapidly. 'Got to go, Mum. This is it.' I gave her a hug, climbed aboard, lowered the window and leant out. She smiled up at me, sharing my excitement.

'Bye, love. Enjoy yourself, and don't forget to write.'

Printed in Great Britain
by Amazon

61093749R00112